BADGER THURSTON
and the
Trouble at the Rodeo

By
Gus Brackett

Illustrations by
Don Gill

To Brayden

Let 'er buck,

Gus Brackett

Twelve Baskets Book Publishing
Three Creek, Idaho

Twelve Baskets Book Publishing, LLC
54899 Crawfish Rd.
Rogerson ID 83302
www.badgerthurston.com
12bookbaskets@gmail.com

ISBN 978-0-9841876-4-5

Author photo by Jill Davidson, Emotion Portrait Design
Edited by Dawn Geluso & Courtenay Edlehart
Cover Design by Chantel Miller

Other books in this series:
Badger Thurston and the Cattle Drive
Badger Thurston and the Runaway Stagecoach
Badger Thurston and the Mud Pits

Table of Contents

Illustrations

Map

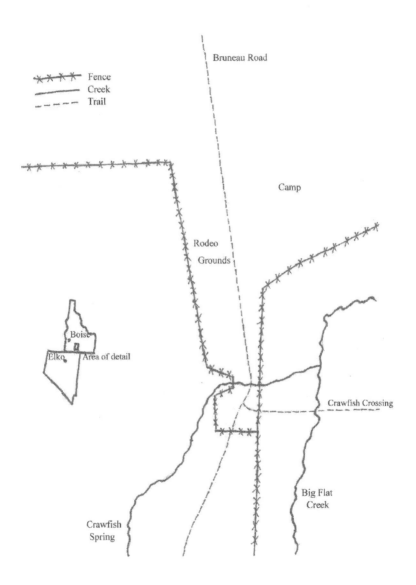

Fence
Creek
Trail

Bruneau Road

Camp

Rodeo
Grounds

Boise
Elko Area of detail

Crawfish Crossing

Big Flat
Creek

Crawfish
Spring

From the author...

Today, a rodeo is a sporting event in which cowboy and animal athletes compete in a variety of Western-style events. In 1910, a rodeo was much different. Back then a rodeo (pronounced ro-DEER in the Northwest) usually happened in the spring. All the ranches in an area would graze cattle on the same ranges without any fences to keep the herds separate. When the grazing season ended, ranchers would gather all the cattle together and separate theirs from the group herd. It was quite a social event for any community. The rodeo described in this book is an old-fashioned, 1910-style rodeo, unlike a rodeo of today.

Chapter One

BADGER SITS TALL IN the saddle and looks over the sagebrush-covered plain. His horse's ears are perked forward, and the beast snorts at an imaginary demon.

"Easy, Blue," Badger says to calm his horse. The young colt is light gray with dark freckles all over his body. With the cloud cover, the horse almost looks blue.

Badger looks up at the clouds rolling in. *I hope I can get these cows back to the rodeo before the wind picks up,* Badger thinks.

Badger and his horse jog around about a dozen cows. Badger yells to get the cows moving, spooking Blue. Badger sits deep in his saddle and squeezes with his knees. The horse tucks his tail and lunges three powerful jumps.

"Easy, Blue," Badger says again, this time to calm himself more than the horse.

Badger pulls the left rein, and the colt jumps in a tight circle. Losing control, Badger's legs and arms tense. The colt can feel Badger's fear and that scares Blue even more.

The colt spooks at a sagebrush and stares with wide, frightened eyes that almost tremble. A breeze shakes the brush leaves. Blue's ears perk forward, and his nostrils flare with fear.

"Stop it, Blue," Badger complains.

Badger pulls on the left rein again and pulls his nervous horse in a tight circle. A gust of wind shakes all the sagebrush branches, and Blue shies to the right like a little boy after you sneak up and scare him.

Badger touches his right spur to Blue's flank. The startled horse jumps to the left and rears up on his back legs like he's dancing a tango.

"Easy, Blue!"

Blue tucks his tail tightly against his rump and runs. The wind whistles in Badger's face. He pulls his hat down tight and grabs the saddle horn on the front of his saddle. With one rein slack, Blue drops his head and bucks.

Blue's back legs kick out, and Badger flails above him. The horse lands hard and jumps again and again, bashing Badger's rump and thighs on the saddle before the young cowboy's feet fly out of the stirrups and he sails through the air like a circus acrobat—until he eats dirt.

Pain shoots through Badger's body. He can't breathe, and he spits out chalky dirt. In a few moments, his lungs relax, and he gulps some air.

Badger sits up and sees Blue racing over the hill, a rooster tail of dust following him. The teen watches his saddle, coat, and ride home disappear over the horizon. Badger pulls his hat off and slaps it against his knee.

Badger stands, picks some stickers out of his hands, dusts some dirt and sagebrush off his chaps and vest, and then wipes a little blood off his cheek. His eyes sting with unshed tears.

Don't get bucked off, Badger remembers Charlie saying. *It's a long walk back to the rodeo grounds.*

Badger's feet hurt as he thinks about it. He shivers as a breeze brushes past, reminding him of the windstorm rolling in.

I wish I had my coat, Badger thinks as he hugs himself for warmth, *and I wish I had my horse.* Badger pulls off his boot, shakes out a pebble, and puts the boot back on. With a sigh and a slight limp, Badger steps toward the horizon.

BADGER'S FEET HURT. HE has a tiny hole in his boot that little rocks sneak in through. He's limping and can feel a bruise forming on his knee from his fall. As the sun ducks behind a cloud, Badger spots a coyote not forty paces from him. It's stalking him, eyeing him from behind a patch of sagebrush.

"I'm not dyin' yet!" Badger yells at the coyote. "You can't eat me!"

Badger picks up a rock and hurls it toward the scavenger. The timid coyote retreats about one hundred yards and then stalks Badger again. The coyote isn't vicious like a wolf; it's more like a stray dog just beyond the reach of the city dogcatcher.

As Badger gimps toward the rodeo grounds, he sees a rider and two horses on the horizon. One of the horses looks like Blue.

"I'm over here!" Badger bellows as he unties his scarf and waves it wildly over his head.

The rider and horses turn north and nearly crest the next hill. *He can't see me*, Badger thinks. *I'm gettin' left behind!*

Badger shuffles like a peg-legged pirate toward the horses, frantically waving his scarf and shouting, "WAIT! I'M HERE! OVER HERE! I DON'T WANNA BE COYOTE DINNER!"

Just before the rider drops out of sight, he stops and looks straight at Badger. The rider turns and jogs the horses toward Badger.

Badger slows and gasps for air. He bends over and grabs his knees. Badger waves his scarf one more time to make sure the rider sees him before pulling off his boot and shaking out more pebbles.

The rider, whose skin is as dark as a moonless midnight, waves with a rein in his hand. His brown eyes crinkle and his white teeth shine as he smiles.

"Boy, am I glad to see you, Charlie," Badger says.

Charlie is a big, strong man. If he stood really still, he would look like one of those fancy Greek statues. Charlie smiles out the side of his mouth, taking in Badger's dirt-smeared face and scraped-up palms. "It's a bad place to lose a horse, cowboy," Charlie says in a deep Texas drawl. He strokes a few stray hairs from his thick mustache. "Y'all better like walkin' if ya can't keep yer backside in the saddle."

"I don't know what happened," Badger says. "Blue has never tried to buck before. I didn't think he had it in him."

"I didn't think he had it in him either," Charlie says. Charlie loosens the cinch around Blue's belly and slides his rough, scarred hand under the saddle blanket. He switches to the other side and stops about halfway back. Charlie pulls something out and inspects it.

"What is it, Charlie?" Badger asks.

"There's a burr under yer saddle blanket," Charlie says.

"A burr? Would a burr make him buck like that?"

"I do declare it'd make me buck," Charlie says.

"How did I get a burr under my saddle blanket?"

"Well, if y'all were sloppy throwin' yer rig on this mornin', it could have stuck to yer blanket."

"I thought I was pretty careful," Badger says. "I did it just like you showed me."

"Regardless of how y'all picked up a burr, we need to get these cows down to the rodeo grounds."

"D-D-D-Do you think Blue's gonna buck again?" Badger asks.

"A horse can buck anytime, usually when ya least expect it," Charlie says. "But he doesn't have a burr under his saddle blanket, and his buck and run tired him out. As long as y'all stay calm and relaxed, ya should be fine."

Calm and relaxed? Badger thinks. *How can I be calm and relaxed after he tossed me off like a rag doll? If Blue won't cooperate, I'm not good enough of a rider to keep my backside in the saddle.*

Badger takes a deep breath. He walks to his horse and strokes the colt's neck a couple times.

"Easy, boy," Badger says, maybe more to himself than to Blue.

Badger measures his reins so that the reins reach the saddle horn with just a little slack. With his reins just the right length, Badger grabs a handful of Blue's coarse mane. The teen slides his left foot into the stirrup and swings into the saddle. Badger wiggles his boot toe into the right stirrup and remeasures his reins.

"Ready to go?" Charlie asks.

Badger nods, but he looks like he just saw a ghost.

"Just relax," Charlie says to Badger. "If you're scared, he'll be scared."

"I'll try."

"Let's round up the cows again and get them down to the rodeo grounds," Charlie says before leading the way.

BADGER AND CHARLIE CREST a slight horizon and the rodeo grounds open up before them. The morning's clouds have moved on, and the bright sun beats down on the land.

Dust boils up from the hundreds of cows and calves lazing together in a single herd. The rodeo grounds are an open area along a single barbed-wire fence. The fence runs for about a half-mile, but the rodeo only takes up a hundred yards or so.

In any other week, the rodeo grounds would look as wide open as all the range surrounding it, but this week it is bustling with activity. With the fence on one side, cowboys on horses stand around the herd to keep the cows together. The cows circle and mill about like a school of fish in a shallow pond.

One cowboy on a particularly athletic horse rides slowly into the herd. He finds a certain cow and calf and separates them from the herd. The rider takes special care to keep the cow and calf together as they wind through cows and calves and bulls to the edge of the herd.

If the cowboy is skilled and in the right position, the cow and calf he wants seep out of the herd and lazily stroll to a second, smaller herd. But if the cow is scared or stubborn, she will try to return to the herd. The rider and horse will shadow the cow back and forth to keep her out. All of this must be done without disturbing the herd. The dance is graceful but can slip into chaos quickly.

This dance happens over and over again as Badger and Charlie follow their cows to the big herd. Beyond the rodeo grounds, six wagons sit in a disorganized circle around a series of campfires. Pots of stew and spits of small game cook on the fires, and every fire has a pot of coffee brewing in it. Only a few cooks and some small children inhabit the wagon city. Everyone else is on horseback either at the rodeo grounds or to the north, trailing more cows in.

Charlie wears the biggest hat I've ever seen, Badger thinks. *Its bright white color looks great against his black skin. He must love that hat because his shirt and pants aren't nearly as spiffy.*

Charlie's plaid shirt is old but well kempt. His pants are faded and well worn, but not tattered. Charlie wears leather cuffs and chaps longer than anyone else's. Everything is bigger with Charlie.

"Boy, I sure do love a rodeo," Charlie says with a grin plastered across his face. His dark eyes gleam with excitement as he rides lazily next to Badger.

"That's what everyone keeps sayin'," Badger says. "Why does everybody get so excited? It's just another day of work."

"Just another day!" Charlie exclaims quietly. "Why, the rodeo for me is like Christmas for a little kid."

"Why?"

"It's the first spring gatherin'," Charlie says. "I'll see folks here I haven't seen since the snow first came."

"That's it?" Badger asks. "Why don't they just have a dance or a potluck? That's a good reason to get together."

"This is yer first rodeo, isn't it?" Charlie asks.

"I really don't know what we're doin' here," Badger says.

"Well, it's simple, Badger," Charlie explains. "All this big, flat, wide-open desert is open range. Anybody with cows can graze 'em out here."

"For free?" Badger asks.

"Nobody owns it, so there's nobody to pay even if they wanted to," Charlie says. "So all the ranchers on Flat Creek, Cherry Creek, and Three Creek have cows rangin' together out here."

"How many are there?" Badger asks.

"There's usually between eight and ten ranches around here, dependin' on who didn't make it through the winter and who moved in."

"And all their cows graze together?"

"That's right—until the rodeo," Charlie says. "'Bout this time every year, everyone in the area gathers all the cows together, and all the ranchers sort out their cows from the common herd. Then everyone goes their separate ways until next spring."

"So why are we here?" Badger asks. "The Shoesole Ranch is fifty miles away."

"The headquarters are fifty miles away," Charlie replies. "Colonel McGill has cattle everywhere though. He owns close to thirty thousand head, so we graze cows wherever we can find extra grass."

"So we're just here to get the colonel's cows off this range? I'm not sure what the excitement is."

"It's more than that," Charlie says. "After the work's done in the afternoon, we have competitions—see who can ride a bronc best, who can rope best. I'm a fair hand at both."

"I guess I'll just have to see it myself," Badger says as a lone rider approaches them.

The lanky rider, Gib Roy, moves easily on the back of his horse.

Badger grins as he remembers working with Gib at the colonel's ranch. Gib was so busy staring at the colonel's daughter that he stepped in the campfire. The coffee pot got stuck on his boot, and he kicked hot coals in every direction, almost burning down the barn. Badger chuckles. *Gib is awkward on the ground and around people,* he thinks. *But on a horse, he's flawless.*

"Hey, Charlie, Badger," the young cowboy says.

"What's the story, Gib?" Charlie asks as they pull their horses to a stop.

"I've got some bad news," Gib says with a grimace as he pulls off his big, brown cowboy hat and runs his hand through his wavy, brown hair. His bright red scarf flaps in the wind, and his brown chaps and vest are coated in a fine dust.

"It can't be that bad," Charlie says, leaning forward and resting his elbows on his saddle horn.

"We've got four neighbors mad at us because their calves have our brand on 'em," Gib says.

"Say what?" Charlie asks, jerking his head back and blinking hard.

"Nearly twenty calves in the herd that have our brand aren't ours," Gib says.

"So four ranchers think we're tryin' to steal their calves?" Badger asks.

"Yep," Gib says, "but it looks like someone used a runnin' iron."

"What's a runnin' iron?" Badger asks.

"Most calves are branded with a brandin' iron," Charlie explains. "The whole pattern is on a single iron, the whole thing is heated, and ya just slap it on. But a runnin' iron is a single bar ya use to draw the brand onto a calf. Outlaws use runnin' irons to rustle cattle."

"Rustle?" Badger asks.

"To steal. Cattle rustlers steal cattle," Charlie explains.

"The Shoesole brand is pretty hard to make with a runnin' iron," Gib explains. "But somebody did it, and it looks close enough to get our neighbors mad."

"Well, we'll get these cows to the herd and get it all straightened out," Charlie says.

"I hope we can," Gib says.

Chapter 2

THERE IS NO WIND, but dust stirs in every direction. The morning storm brought only wind, so the afternoon ground is even drier. The cows at the rodeo grounds are together in a circling herd. Some cows stand calmly and chew their cud.

With all the activity, many of the pairs become separated, so those cows circle the herd looking for their missing calves. The cows on the move stir up most of the dust. The rodeo ground is surprisingly loud. About half the cows cannot find their calves, and all those cows and calves moo loudly in their search. The resulting symphony is noisy and chaotic.

Charlie waves a greeting as he rides up to the herd. Four riders approach from the rodeo. The three older men and one woman ride with the authority of ranch owners or cow bosses.

"Howdy, Charlie," a man with a salt-and-pepper beard says as they approach. "We've got a bit of a problem."

"Well, I'm sure whatever the problem is we can find a fix for it, Mr. Strickland," Charlie says. His smile is disarming, so he keeps it plastered from cheek to cheek. A second man with a bushy, gray mustache and a short-brimmed hat looks like a teapot just before it boils. His angry eyes glare at Charlie.

"You've been stealin' calves from all four of us," the gray-haired man sneers.

"Now Mr. Winters, there is a big difference between an honest mistake and a thievin' crime."

"Five of my calves have your brand on 'em!" Fred Winters almost yells. "And it's a fresh brand, about a week old."

"Now I know we can fix this," Charlie says. "We have a couple dozen unbranded calves. We could put your brand on 'em, and then we'd be even. How many calves are carryin' the wrong brand?"

"Five of my calves," Mr. Winters says, "and I'm not takin' any of your dinks."

"No, sir," Charlie says. "It would be yer pick of our best."

"There's just three of mine," Homer Strickland says. "Your solution is more than fair."

"And Mrs. Salles, how many for y'all?"

"Six of our calves carry your brand," says Laura Salles. "But two of 'em are pretty sickly. I'm not sure they're gonna live. You don't have to replace those two."

"No, ma'am," Charlie says. "When we get our cows sorted out, we'll stoke up the fire and brand six of our calves with yer brand. And how 'bout y'all, Mr. Caudle?"

The sad-faced Mr. Caudle doesn't speak a word. He just raises two fingers.

"We'll get two of our best for ya then," Charlie says like a doctor comforting his patient.

Everyone nods in agreement. Charlie scans the herd of cattle to see the brand in question. As he looks, Mr. Winters pulls close to Charlie.

"I'm sure disappointed," Mr. Winters snarls. "I've always know Colonel McGill to be an honest man, but I guess this is what happens when he hires a black man for his cow boss. I don't know if you folks are crooked or just sloppy. Either way, it reflects poorly on the colonel."

Charlie ignores the comment. He's heard variations of it lots of times before. Charlie squints as he spots one of the calves in question. Charlie shakes his head as he sees the brand on the left rib.

"I don't think we're bein' sloppy, Mr. Winters," Charlie says as he gestures to the calf. "I think we're bein' set up."

"Whattaya mean?" Mr. Strickland asks.

"These calves have been branded with a runnin' iron," Charlie says, "and ya said the brand was from 'bout a week ago."

"That's what I said," Mr. Winters says, less angrily. "What's your point?"

"We pulled in here two days ago," Charlie says with a grin. "The last three weeks, we had a camp over in the Basin. That's three days' ride from here. That's our brand all right, but that's not our handiwork."

Charlie tips his hat back and wipes sweat from his forehead.

"So who's tryin' to set you up?" Mrs. Salles asks.

"That's my question too," Charlie says. "I don't know who would do such a thing—or why. But I'm fixin' to find out."

"I don't like to point fingers," Mr. Strickland says, "but those Joiner brothers have been stirrin' up trouble."

"They came down to my place three days ago and opened the gate on my horses," Mrs. Salles says. "I walked more than a mile to get my first horse back. I don't mind a good prank, but their pranks are just plain mean."

"We'll worry 'bout the whos and whys later," Charlie says. "Right now we have cows to sort."

All five turn around and ride back to the herd. The cows and calves have settled down and many have lain down. The six cowboys surrounding the herd fidget like five-year-olds in the third hour of church. Some lean forward, propping their heads on their hands. Others have dismounted and are adjusting their saddles or chaps or other parts of their rig.

Mr. Caudle rides into the herd and most of the other cowboys spring to life. They tighten their cinches and climb on their horses. Some of the cowboys look attentive and ready to work. The rest still look bored.

Mr. Caudle finds one of his cows and her calf and guides them to the edge of the herd. They calmly mosey out of the herd and down the fence. Mr. Caudle is very crafty and cuts the cows out with very little movement.

Badger settles at the edge of the herd between Charlie and Gib. He is sore all over. His backside is sore from sitting. His front side is sore from falling off his horse. His head throbs, and he's thirsty.

Holdin' herd is the most borin' job ever created, he thinks.

After about an hour, Mr. Caudle looks through the herd one more time. He jogs his horse down to the smaller herd and counts the cows of his that he has sorted out. As he wanders back to the rodeo grounds, Charlie and the other ranchers join him in another meeting.

"How many cows are y'all short?" Charlie asks.

Mr. Caudle shakes his head and lifts one finger in the air.

"Well that other one is bound to turn up," Charlie says. "When she does, I'll make sure she makes it over to yer place."

Mr. Caudle nods at Charlie, and his sad face shoots a quick half smile.

"Y'all sure yer not gonna stay for all the fun tonight?" Charlie asks.

Mr. Caudle shakes his head and nods toward his ranch.

"Can I help move yer cows through the gate then?" Charlie asks.

Mr. Caudle grins and nods.

The two cowboys roust the lazy cows and calves and follow them to the gate. Just as the first cow reaches the gate, two riders jog up a small hill and stand in the way. The lead cow shies and turns to run. The rest of the cows fall in behind her like dominoes. The small herd stampedes back toward the large herd. Nearly all the cowboys race to that side to keep the cows from mixing and wasting an afternoon of work.

Charlie races around the small herd and turns the lead cow back toward the gate. The rest of the herd dutifully follows. Charlie stops to let the agitated cows calm down.

The two riders are still standing in the gateway. One is readjusting his saddle as the other rider looks on.

It looks like they're standin' in the way on purpose, Badger thinks, *just to be annoyin'*.

Finally, the cowboy clambers back into his saddle and the two riders saunter off. With the roadblock moved, the cows with their calves trailing neatly behind them walk through the opening. Charlie tips his hat to Mr. Caudle and closes the gate.

As Charlie rides back toward the big herd of cows, the two cowboys who caused the ruckus sidle up close to Badger, who holds herd on the southern side alone. The taller, lanky one is on his left and the shorter, stocky rider is on his right.

"Howdy, greenhorn," the stocky one says. "What's your name?"

"Badger, Badger Thurston."

"Okay, Badger Badger Thurston," the rider says as he leans forward and rests his elbow on his saddle horn. "I'm Hark Joiner, and that's my baby brother, Harlan."

Harlan grins a stupid grin and chuckles. "Badger Badger Thurston."

"Did you get the flower I sent you, greenhorn?" Hank asks.

"What flower?" Badger asks. He tilts his head like a curious calf.

"I left it under your saddle blanket this mornin'," Hank says with a fiendish smirk.

"You put the burr under my saddle blanket?" Badger asks. "Why would you do that?"

Harlan leans in close to Badger and repeats in his stupid voice, "Why would you do that?"

"Don't take it personal, Badger Badger Thurston," Hank says with a strange, angry look in his eye. "Our job is to get rid of all the Shoesole Ranch cowboys. Now you could make our job easy and just leave. Or you can stay, and we'll beat you uglier than you already are."

"Well, I hired on with Charlie," Badger says. "I can't just leave. I'm—"

Hank snatches Badger by the collar and tugs. Badger wobbles to the side and flops to the ground for the second time that day.

Harlan snaps his reins like a whip, smacking Blue's rump. Blue sticks his tail in the air and runs to the north like a lion is chasing him. He tops the horizon and streaks out of sight.

"Wrong answer, Badger Badger Thurston," Hank spits with the same angry look. "You and the others from the Shoesole better get while you still can."

Badger sits up and wipes dirt from his face. He's a little surprised and a little winded, so he doesn't say anything.

The Joiner brothers spur their horses and wander lazily to the cows coming into the herd.

Badger slowly rises and dusts himself off. He has a rip in his shirt and little pebbles have already wormed their way into Badger's boot.

Walkin' again. Badger shakes his head as he follows Blue's path toward the horizon. *Why are those Joiners pickin' on me? What did they mean that we gotta leave?*

BADGER LIMPS A LITTLE on his left foot. Blisters have erupted on his big toe and heel, and they burn. He stops and shakes the pebbles out of his boot again, but two steps later they're back.

With about a half mile of trail behind him, Badger sees Charlie riding his horse and leading Blue. Badger breathes a sigh to break the pressure. He tips his hat back and wipes sweat off his dusty forehead.

Charlie grins as he approaches. "Blue should be aired out now, Badger," Charlie says.

"You're probably gettin' sick of chasin' my horse down," Badger says as he accepts his reins from Charlie.

"I was the new kid once," Charlie says. "I fell off my horse more than my fair share. Somebody always brought my pony back to me. I track yer horse down to repay 'em just as much as I do it for y'all."

"I appreciate it," Badger says as he measures his reins and pulls his stirrup around. Badger slips his foot into the stirrup and hesitates before swinging onto Blue. The colt is still breathing heavily.

"Why would the Joiner brothers want all of us who ride for the Shoesole Ranch to leave?" Badger asks.

"They want us outta here? Huh," Charlie says. "I don't know why, but we better figure it out quick."

Badger swings onto Blue, and the two cowboys walk their horses back toward the rodeo. Both beasts are tired and sweaty as racehorses, and both cowboys are the same. Dust is kicked up with every step, and it seems like all the dust ends up on their faces.

"We better hurry back," Charlie says as the rodeo grounds come into view. "They're probably done sortin' for today."

"If they're done, what's the hurry?" Badger asks.

"Once the work's all done, then the fun starts."

"What's planned for tonight?"

"We usually do some bronc ridin' the first night," Charlie says. "The horses always buck harder before they get tuckered out."

"Will you ride a bronc tonight?" Badger asks.

"I will if y'all will help me get aboard."

"I'll help," Badger says.

Charlie smiles a big toothy grin.

"Which horse will you ride?" Badger asks.

"Well, I'll bring that old gray mare named Marianne," Charlie says.

"You mean the one that stands in the corner and kicks anybody who gets close?" Badger asks. "I don't understand why such a mean old mare has a pretty name like Marianne."

"She was named after the colonel's mother-in-law. Trust me; the name fits."

"So you'll ride Marianne?" Badger asks.

"No, another bronc buster from another outfit will ride Marianne," Charlie explains, "and I'll ride a renegade horse from some other outfit. If I can ride the other guy's meanest bronc better than he can ride our meanest horse, then I'll be the winner."

"I don't think I'd like to try that," Badger says as he brushes a weed off his chaps. "But I'd like to see it."

"Y'all have a front-row seat," Charlie says. "I need a flanker."

"A what?" Badger asks.

"A flanker," Charlie says. "Y'all see when we get started."

Chapter 3

THE SUN HANGS LOW in the western sky. All the cow work is done, and dinner is cooking on a shared fire with five cooks lounging behind six buckaroo wagons. One cook darts about the fire like a hummingbird gathering nectar as he tends to a meal for fifty people. The five other cooks drink coffee and relax, knowing that soon they'll take their turns around the campfire.

The herd's cows begin streaming away from the rodeo grounds. The cows will find their calves, eat some grass, and drink some muddy water. Cowboys will gather up the cows again tomorrow and the next day and the next until all the ranchers' herds are separate. The range will rest and regrow until next spring's grazing season, when all the area ranchers will again graze their cows together on this range.

Most of the cowboys are unsaddling their horses and tending to other chores around the wagons. There is sagebrush and dried cow patties to gather to fuel the fires. Some cowboys repair minor damage to their gear. Others relax and drink warm cups of coffee.

A few kids play with the only toys they have— lariats. They rope sagebrush, rocks, saddles, each other, and anything else that moves. Most of their mothers are back at their homesteads, and most of their fathers are catching up on gossip around the campfire.

As Charlie and Badger approach the wagons, a grin creeps across Charlie's face.

"What is it?" Badger asks.

"Over there." Charlie points toward the remuda where the horses graze and rest.

Badger watches with widening blue eyes as three stubborn men lead three angry horses out of the remuda herd and toward the wagons. These three beasts balk, kick, stomp, and strain against their handlers.

"They're gettin' ready for the bronc ridin'," Charlie says before beaming like a good little boy on Christmas morning.

"Are we too late?" Badger asks. "What about Marianne?"

"Gib is just now leadin' her out," Charlie says as he points to the gray mare reluctantly tethered to Gib.

Gib holds on with both hands. Every time the lead rope comes tight, Marianne shakes her head and neck side to side and lunges forward. Before she hits the ground, she paws at Gib. With this clunky shake-lunge-paw, Gib and Marianne follow the other horses to a wide open spot.

Badger and Charlie arrive at nearly the same time. Charlie quickly dismounts and strips the saddle off his horse. He whips the hobbles out of a D-ring on the back of the saddle and secures the hobbles around his horse's front legs. Badger hobbles Blue but leaves him saddled. With the horses hobbled so they don't wander far, Badger and Charlie stroll to the circle of competitors.

Mr. Strickland holds four sticks in his hand, one for each competitor.

"Longest stick gets to pick first," Mr. Strickland explains. "Shortest stick picks last."

Pat O'Brien pulls the first stick. It's about medium length. Harlan Joiner pulls the next stick, and it's shorter than Mr. O'Brien's. Charlie pulls next, and his stick is by far the shortest. Mr. Strickland opens his palm to reveal the longest stick.

Mr. Strickland surveys the sticks. "Looks like I'm first, Pat is second, Harlan is third, and Charlie is last."

Mr. Strickland takes a quick look at the four horses and chooses the sway-backed brown horse Mr. O'Brien brought. The brown appears to be the friendliest of the mean horses.

Two of Mr. Strickland's hired hands help get the beast saddled. One man holds the rope tightly, and the other holds the horse's head. Mr. Strickland throws his saddle on and pulls the straps through and tight. The horse glares angrily at Mr. Strickland but doesn't resist the saddle.

Mr. Strickland raises his left foot to the stirrup. With a handful of mane in his left hand, he swings onto the annoyed bronc. He wiggles to the left and the right and finds his perfect spot. His hired hand tosses the lead rope up to Mr. Strickland just as the rancher cries through bared teeth, "Lemme have him!"

The man holding the horse's head lets go and runs the short distance back to the wagons. All fifty people in the camp watch breathlessly as the horse eyes the wide open rodeo grounds. The horse rears on his hind legs and lunges to his right. Mr. Strickland sticks to his saddle like he's glued there. The horse lands on his front hooves and a cloud of dust rises off the hairy beast.

The horse bunches his legs beneath him and bucks high in the air. The brim of Mr. Strickland's hat flips straight in the air, but he remains seated comfortably in the saddle. The horse kicks his hooves high to the sky, but Mr. Strickland doesn't budge.

The brown nimbly gathers his hooves and jumps like a jack rabbit. The horse rolls his back to the right and kicks his hooves high to the left. The horse lands hard on all four hooves, and Mr. Strickland absorbs the shock sitting deep in the saddle.

And then the horse stops, and the brim on Mr. Strickland's hat flips back down to its normal position. The bronc breathes heavily through flared nostrils, and the still-gathering crowd collectively exhales and cheers. Mr. Strickland jabs his spurs into the horse's flank, but the winded horse is spent. He kicks two more times and, satisfied that the ride is over, Mr. Strickland swings his leg over the cantle and drops to the ground.

"Is that the roughest horse you've got, Pat?" Mr. Strickland asks.

"Old Two Jumps is the only one I have that bucks," Mr. O'Brien replies. "I have a whole string of horses that won't buck."

"That's a good string, I guess," Mr. Strickland says. "A little borin', but a good string. Well, you're up next, Pat."

"I'll ride the horse you brought, Homer," Mr. O'Brien says with a confident grin. "Can I borrow your muggers?"

"Sure can," Mr. Strickland says. "My boys know a few tricks to get a saddle on Old Bandit."

MR. STRICKLAND'S HIRED HANDS walk the horse away from the spectators and wagons. The black gelding strains against the lead rope and strikes at the cowboys with his black hooves. Mr. Strickland's horse has a white blaze on his forehead just below both eyes, so he looks like a bandit with a mask covering his face.

The second hired hand sneaks up the rope and slides a wild rag over Old Bandit's eyes. Like a caged bird in the dark, the black horse stands still and calm.

Mr. O'Brien throws his saddle on Old Bandit. With shaking hands, the rancher pulls the leather latigoes through the D-rings and cinches the saddle down tight like pulling on a shoe's laces.

Mr. O'Brien gingerly places his foot in the stirrup, hesitates, and then cautiously swings into the saddle. One hired hand slides the rope up to Mr. O'Brien while the other continues to cover Old Bandit's eyes.

"Are you ready?" the hired hand covering the horse's eyes asks.

"Almost," Mr. O'Brien says. "Not quite yet."

He measures the rope in his hand and sinks deeper into his saddle. He takes a breath and remeasures the rope.

"Are you ready?" the mugger asks again.

"Not quite—almost," Mr. O'Brien says.

"You're ready!" the hired hand demands.

"Okay, I'm ready," Mr. O'Brien says through gritted teeth. "Let him have me!"

The cowboy steps back, pulling off the rag. Old Bandit blinks twice. Mr. O'Brien squints, his face frozen in a flinch like a miner whose dynamite is about to explode.

Like a burning fuse finally hitting the blasting cap, the black gelding lunges forward. Mr. O'Brien slides out of his saddle but catches up quickly to the bucking horse. Old Bandit's front hooves hit the ground, and Mr. O'Brien lurches forward. His backside lifts out of the saddle, and he bumps hard into the cantle. The horse bucks forward again, and Mr. O'Brien slams into his saddle. He leans to his left and grabs his rope to keep his balance.

As Old Bandit soars high in the air, Mr. O'Brien's foot slips out of the right stirrup. The black gelding's front hooves hit the earth, stopping abruptly. But Mr. O'Brien keeps moving forward—and splats on the ground.

The black gelding gathers his hooves and lunges forward again with his rider beneath his hooves. Mr. O'Brien, lying in a heap on the ground, sighs in relief as Old Bandit bucks away without stomping on him.

"Two jumps, Pat?" Mr. Strickland asks. "That's all you've got, two jumps?"

"That's why the horse I brought stops after two jumps. I'm only good for two jumps," Mr. O'Brien says as he shakes dirt out of his pants pocket. "I think it's safe to say I'm in second place after two riders."

Everyone within earshot laughs. Mr. Strickland helps Mr. O'Brien up and they walk back to the cowboys.

"You're next, Harlan," Mr. Strickland says. "Only one horse is left you can choose."

"I'll ride my own horse," Harlan says with an eye roll and half grin.

"Now wait a minute," Mr. O'Brien says. "It's customary to ride a horse from a different outfit, so you can prove your mettle."

"I'm not ridin' that gray from the Shoesole Ranch," Harlan says with a sneer.

"A lot of people are scared of Marianne," Charlie says, "but she's a sweet ride."

"He's not scared," Hank says, defending his brother. "He just won't ride a horse a monkey's ridden."

"Uh, oh," Charlie says with a smile. "Is my tail showing?"

Everyone laughs at Charlie's joke, grateful to him for breaking the tension.

Hank is bein' hateful for no reason, Badger thinks. *But Charlie doesn't even blink; he just makes a joke outta a bad situation.*

"Well, he won't ride the gray," Hank says.

"Then he won't ride," Mr. Strickland responds.

The Joiner brothers suddenly mount up, spin around, and gallop away with their bronc trailing behind.

"There goes my horse," Charlie says as deflated as a cooled-off hot-air balloon. "I guess that means I'm outta the contest."

"Sorry, Charlie," Mr. Strickland says. "It kinda ruins the party without you ridin' in the contest."

Charlie tilts his head and ponders for a moment. His eyes light up. Charlie extends his hand to Mr. Strickland and they shake. "Congratulations on winnin' the bronc bustin'," Charlie says loud enough for everyone to hear. Then he quietly turns to Mr. Strickland and says, "but I need the practice, so I'm gonna take Marianne for a spin."

The onlookers clap and hoot for the victor. The applause wanes, and attention shifts to the aroma wafting from the cook fires.

"Before you grab your grub," Mr. Strickland says, "Charlie's gonna take a spin on his gray mare, if you wanna watch."

The spectators sit back down on the dirt near the wagons. Gib hands the lead rope to Badger, and Badger holds it like it's a rattlesnake.

"You have to hold on tighter than that," Gib says to Badger. "If you let go, Charlie's as good as a ship in a storm without an anchor."

Gib walks toward Marianne with his hand on the rope. She lurches backward and tugs at Badger's arms. He almost loses his grip, so he wraps a half twist around his waist for leverage. Gib walks the remaining three steps down the rope, calmly whispering to Marianne. Gib pulls the scarf from his neck and drapes it over Marianne's eyes. Gib secures the scarf under her throat and then slings his arm over her neck and grabs onto her ear with his fingers.

Marianne rears on her back legs and paws at the air with her front hooves, but with Badger on the rope and Gib on her neck, she can't resist so she stands still. Her ears are pinned back and her nostrils flare. Her flank shudders with every breath.

With a big, toothy grin, Charlie walks up to Badger.

He raises his eyebrows at Badger and says, "Just hold on, Badger. When I get in the saddle, throw me the rope."

"Sure, Charlie," Badger says through gritted teeth as he strains to hold onto the rope.

Charlie saunters to the renegade horse, keeping one hand on the rope. Marianne shakes her head from side to side. Gib holds onto her head, and Badger tightens his grip. Charlie pets Marianne on the nose, and her ears perk forward. Her whole body quivers with anger. Charlie gently slides his hand down her neck to her withers. In one easy motion, Charlie swings the saddle onto her back and slides it tight against her withers. Charlie is as relaxed as Marianne is angry.

Charlie reaches his hand under her belly and pulls the braided wool cinch to the leather latigo. Drips of sweat gather on Charlie's bushy black mustache. His expert hands wind the latigo through the D-ring and pull the cinch down tight. Marianne squats on her back legs and strikes at Charlie's boot-long chaps. Charlie looks up from beneath his oversized cowboy hat and takes a deep breath.

Badger's arms ache, and his hands are blistering.

"Almost ready?" Gib asks. "I think she's about ready to blow her top."

Charlie nods and slides his left boot into the stirrup. He jumps once and swings his leg over the cantle and into the right stirrup. He slides down low into the saddle.

"Throw me the rope, Badger," Charlie yells as his calm demeanor finally wavers.

Badger throws the rope and runs. Charlie snags it with his left hand. He winds the thick rope between his pinky and ring finger, gripped with his middle three fingers, and the tail of the rope hangs between his thumb and fingers.

"Let 'er buck!" Charlie yells to Gib.

Gib releases Marianne, pulling the scarf away as he dashes back. Marianne paws at Gib as he runs back toward the wagons. Charlie hooks his spurs into the big gray's flank.

Marianne drops her head and pulls her hooves together. With one powerful jump, the mare sails through the air with Charlie glued to his seat. Marianne throws her head to the right and her front hoof to the left. As she lands, she twists her back—a move that would send a lesser rider flying, but Charlie sits deep in his saddle. Charlie pulls his feet back and gouges his spurs into Marianne's flank.

With nostrils flared and ears pinned back, Marianne gathers her hooves and bucks again. Charlie barely wavers as he fans his feet forward and back in perfect rhythm with every jump. Charlie's left arm pulls on the lead rope and his right hand clutches his coiled rope strapped to his saddle horn. The onlookers cheer louder and louder with each jump.

Marianne's long mane flows wildly as she turns around and bucks toward the wagons. Charlie has barely moved from his perch. Marianne bucks to within twenty yards of the cheering crowd and then crow hops three times like a kid in a potato-sack race.

The spectators cheer louder, and Charlie pulls his hat off and, showing off a little, smacks Marianne on both sides of her rump. He then flings his hat into the air like a boomerang.

Marianne turns hard on her haunches and takes two more soft jumps. She stops and pants. Charlie touches his spurs to her side, but Marianne concedes victory to Charlie.

The crowd noise reaches a peak and then calms to a couple wild-eyed old-timers clapping just a little bit extra. Then the dull silence of dusk takes over. Charlie pulls Marianne around in a tight circle. The crowd slowly swarms around the boiling pots of food. Most everyone has a plate and either a fork or spoon. With a longing look toward dinner, Badger instead scurries toward Blue and pulls off the colt's hobbles. Gib follows his friend. In the quiet away from the bustle of the crowd, Badger hears a dull roar in the distance. He looks at the gray horizon and squints. Badger sees a plume of dust heading their way, and the roar progressively gets louder.

"Hey, Gib," Badger says as he points toward the cloud. "What's kickin' up that dust?"

Gib turns his head and reflexively yells, "Stampede! Stampede!" And he runs to his horse.

Stampede? Badger thinks. *That can't be good.*

Chapter 4

BLUE'S EYES ARE WIDE open and his ears perk forward. Both his and Badger's hearts race as the sound of the thundering herd gets closer with every second.

Badger measures his reins, steps his left foot into the stirrup, and swings onto his horse. Blue pulls his tail tightly against his rump. Blue takes one little hop, but Badger grabs his left rein and pulls Blue into a tight circle. The colt gives control back to Badger and calms down.

How can I keep Blue calm when I'm this scared? Badger wonders.

The mass of cattle runs closer like a series of waves storming a beach.

As Badger jogs Blue toward the stampede, Charlie gallops Marianne past him. Marianne has all the buck out of her, so she follows Charlie's instructions like a thoroughbred race horse.

I don't know what to do! Badger thinks. *But Charlie does! I'll follow him.* And he and Blue take off toward the herd.

Mr. Strickland rides Old Bandit close on Charlie's heels. Bandit runs and then bucks. Mr. Strickland jams his spurs into Bandit's flanks. Bandit lunges forward, kicks his hind legs out, and then hits the ground running. Bandit still wants to buck, but Mr. Strickland is in a hurry and forces the beast to gallop instead.

Cowboys hurry to strap saddles onto frightened horses. The rest of the camp scurries to secure the wagons and tend to the equipment.

But action is needed now. And only Charlie, Mr. Strickland, and Badger are ready to ride, so it falls to them to try to turn the stampede. Charlie and Marianne speed across the ground like a downhill freight train, reaching the agitated herd first. Charlie veers to the lead flank of the herd.

"WHOOP! HAW!" Charlie bellows.

In the turmoil, only a few cows hear his cry, but those ones turn slightly. Charlie spurs a streaking Marianne forward, waves his free hand, and chirps a whistle. The cows nearest him turn a little bit more.

"HEHAW! WHOA!" Mr. Strickland shouts as he rides directly behind Charlie.

Nearly one hundred cows and calves charge within four hundred yards of the rodeo grounds and wagons. Badger finally catches up and pulls in behind Mr. Strickland. Blue is terrified, and Badger has almost no control over the colt.

Mr. Strickland and Charlie whoop and holler at the edge of the rampaging herd. The cows run blindly and kick up a massive cloud of dust. Hundreds of sharp hooves pound the dirt as the herd rolls closer to the wagons. A few more cowboys are mounted.

In all the commotion, Blue bolts toward the middle of the herd.

"Easy, Blue!" Badger yells as he unsuccessfully pulls on the reins to stop his horse.

The horse and rider lunge into a cow on the edge.

"Whoa, Blue! Whoa!" Badger yells as he pulls on the reins.

Blue wades into the herd like an otter jumping into a pond and the cows scatter. This is just enough to force the lead cows to turn forty-five degrees to the east. Charlie and Mr. Strickland put more pressure on the cattle and they veer farther away.

Gib and several other cowboys arrive and help push the herd just beyond the wagons. The cloud of dust settles on the camp, but all the cows go around the wagons.

Badger finally gets Blue to respond and reins him in. Badger is breathless, and Blue is soaked in sweat. Blue slows to a trot and then a walk and then stops. Blue's flanks heave as the colt tries to catch his breath.

The worst is past as the rest of the cowboys finish turning the herd. And as quickly as it arrived, the stampede slows to a walk and then fizzles out.

BACK AT THE REMUDA, Charlie pulls the saddle off Marianne. Frazzled cowboys tend to their horses or stare blankly at the campfire.

"That was a bold move, Badger," Charlie says loudly. "Y'all probably saved most of the wagons and a couple cowboys by gettin' the herd to turn."

"It wasn't like that," Badger says. "Blue ran away with me, and we bumped into the herd. I was just tryin' to stay on."

"Well, somebody would have hollered at ya if ya were at the wrong place at the wrong time. So I'll give ya an attaboy for bein' in the right place at the right time," Charlie says as he pats Badger on the back.

"Whattaya think spooked 'em?" Gib asks. "There's not a cloud in the sky, and there's no lightnin' or thunder."

"It was those Joiner boys," Mr. Strickland says, wagging his pointer finger. "That's who did it."

"Now let's not jump to hasty conclusions," Charlie says.

"But it's obvious," Mr. Strickland says. "Those Joiner boys leave here angry headed north. And not more than thirty minutes later, we get a stampede from that same direction."

"Startin' a stampede is more effort than I've ever seen those boys put into anythin'," Charlie says. "I'll tell ya, there's somebody else behind all this."

"Well, those boys are gonna get an earful from me when I run across 'em next," Mr. Strickland says, straightening his gloves forcefully before dusting off his well-worn chaps. Mr. Strickland squints his trail-worn eyes and licks his chapped lips.

"They need an earful from somebody," Charlie agrees, "but right now I need a bellyful. Who's hungry?"

The cowboys silently agree and head to the wagons for dinner.

THE DARK MORNING releases just a hint of pink. Everyone is snoring and sleeping like a graveyard's dead except Badger, who wishes he still were.

The second day at the rodeo is always the hardest. All the bumps, bruises, and saddle sores are still fresh, and they all hurt every time Badger moves. But it's Badger's turn to wrangle the horses, so he rolls out of his bedroll. Every bump and bruise from the day before throbs, and Badger stretches to pull some of the ache out.

I should have stayed in school, Badger thinks, *or got a job in town. I'd still be in bed, and I wouldn't be so sore. But I'd be bored and missin' out on the rodeo.*

Badger pulls his shirt and pants over his faded red long johns and then pulls on his brown boots, hat, and vest. He winds his multicolored scarf around his neck and slides into his coat. Badger walks away from the sleeping cowboys to slide into his chaps and clamp on his spurs. He then *jingle-jangle-jingles* into the dawn to find his horse.

Blue is hobbled about fifty yards away. Badger slips the bit into Blue's mouth and slides the headstall over the young horse's ears.

Blue chews on the bit to get it in the right spot and then sticks his tongue out to make sure the bit is really in place.

Badger carefully checks for stickers on his saddle blanket and then throws it on Blue's back. The saddle is next, and Badger screws it on tight. Badger walks in a tight circle with Blue right behind him to get Blue stretched out.

Badger takes a deep breath, gathers his reins and pulls his stirrup up to get on. As Badger raises his leg,

Blue jumps to the side and bucks twice. Badger takes a deep breath to calm down, but it doesn't work. Badger remeasures his reins and steps up close to Blue again. Blue jumps to the side and circles around.

"Hold still, Blue," Badger says loudly, his frustration seething out in his words.

Blue stands, and Badger gets his left foot in the stirrup. Badger pulls up halfway, but Blue spooks and Badger falls to the ground. Blue's eyes bulge and his nostrils flare. His ears perk in several directions as he looks for threats everywhere.

"Stand, Blue!" Badger yells.

Badger steps into the stirrup and quickly swings on. Blue drops his head and bucks twice. Badger, who hasn't quite found the saddle, flies over the front of Blue and lands on the ground—again. Badger quickly jumps to his feet and grabs a rein before Blue can run away. Badger roughly tugs on the rein and Blue spooks but doesn't run away.

"Blue!" Badger yells.

I should still be in bed, Badger thinks. *What am I doin' here? I'm in over my head.*

Badger walks toward Blue, and Blue steps away. Badger takes another step, but Blue won't let Badger anywhere near him.

"STAND STILL, BL—"

"Easy, Badger," Charlie calmly interrupts. Badger jumps when he hears Charlie's voice.

"Take a deep breath," Charlie says as he walks up. Charlie is fresh out of his bedroll. He isn't wearing a shirt or pants. He just has on dirty white long johns, boots, and a cowboy hat.

"Horses are a lot like people," Charlie says as he walks over to Blue. Charlie puts his hand on Blue's nose and then strokes the horse's neck. "They don't do well when people yell at 'em. I won't yell at ya, Badger. Y'all don't yell at yer horse."

"You're right," Badger says with a huff. "Blue is all stirred up. Why won't he just stand? Why does he keep buckin' me off?"

"He's just scared, Badger," Charlie says calmly. "Once he gets scared, ya have to start all over with him gettin' him calmed back down."

Blue nuzzles against Charlie as Charlie strokes his neck. Badger snickers a little because Charlie's talking nice to a horse while standing in just his underwear.

Charlie steps to the side of Blue, puts his foot in the stirrup and swings onto the colt's back.

Blue shakes with fear, and his eyes bulge like a mouse's when a hawk shrieks. Blue drops his head and bucks high in the air. Charlie sits calmly in the saddle. Blue bucks again and then runs out of his buck. When he slows to a jog, Charlie pulls him around. Charlie trots toward the horizon for about a quarter-mile and then turns around and jogs back to Badger.

As they approach, Charlie stops him, backs him up, spins to the right and then spins to the left. With Charlie's guidance, Blue travels like an old-broke reining horse.

"Maybe I should try ridin' in just my underwear," Badger jokes as he admires Charlie's handiwork. Charlie ignores the comment.

"He's all ready for ya, Badger," Charlie says as he swings off Blue. "Give him his head and air him out right when ya get on."

"Thanks, Charlie," Badger says as he steps into the stirrup and swings on.

"The horses probably didn't wander too far off. Y'all should be able to find 'em just over the horizon. Now go get those horses wrangled," Charlie says.

A SMALL HERD MILLS about, its cows looking for their calves. All the cows have the Shoesole brand on their ribs, and most of the calves do too. The sun is just starting to drop. The sky is clear, and the day is hot.

The day's sort is complete, and all the cows except the Shoesole Ranch cows are streaming away like ants from a flooded ant pile.

The Shoesole cows are crowded into a corner of a five-wire, barbed wire fence. Just away from the herd, a small sagebrush-fueled fire burns. Five branding irons glow in the coals. Badger, Gib, and several other ranch hands linger close enough to the fire to be ready to brand the calves, but far enough away to avoid the heat.

Charlie and Mr. Strickland make some final adjustments to their saddled horses. Both cowboys have their rawhide lariats draped over their saddle horns and are ready to rope.

"Are the irons hot?" Mr. Strickland asks.

One of the ranch hands walks to the fire and picks up the 7Z brand with gloved hands. He pulls it out of the fire and inspects the glowing rod of metal.

"Iron's hot," the ranch hand yells back.

Most of the cows and all the calves are mooing, and the symphony fills Badger's ears.

Charlie and Mr. Strickland swing their ropes and ride slowly into the herd. They both search for unbranded calves from the sixty calves in the herd.

Charlie spies the first slick calf, so he swings his loop. He guides his horse, weaving through the cows until he faces the fire and the unbranded calf's hind end faces Charlie's horse on the right side. Charlie swings his loop around and throws the rope to the ground. The rope smacks a back leg of the calf and encircles both legs. With this perfect loop, the calf steps forward into the loop and Charlie pulls the slack on the rope. The loop snares tight, and Charlie spins the rope twice around his saddle horn.

With the lariat secure around the calf's hooves, Charlie turns his horse toward the fire and drags the calf. As Charlie pulls the calf near the fire, two ranch hands jump into action. One grabs the rope, and the other grabs the calf's tail. They both pull at the same time, and the calf falls to the ground. When done correctly like this, the calf drops easily and the other work begins. When done incorrectly, the muggers get kicked, battered, and spend most of the time in the dirt.

Next, one of the ranch hands puts his knee on the ribs of the calf and holds a front leg to keep the calf from moving.

"Brand this one with a rafter-S," Charlie yells to be heard over the lowing cows. "This one and the next two will be for Mr. Strickland."

Gib pulls the rafter-S iron out of the fire and walks the glowing metal to the calf. Gib sets the iron on the calf's right hip. The calf struggles, but Gib holds the iron in place.

Thick smoke roils up as the hair smolders like a dying campfire. After a few seconds, the smoke changes from a greenish gray to a bluish gray and Gib removes the iron to reveal a perfect brown brand. Another man with a knife makes a small notch in the calf's ear and then whittles a waddle on its left hip.

The ranch hand holding the calf looks up at Charlie to make sure the calf is finished, and Charlie nods his approval. The man stands, and Charlie slacks his rope. The calf jumps up and runs back into the herd.

Meanwhile, Mr. Strickland has already secured a calf and taken it to a separate team of branders. Charlie and Mr. Strickland rope and drag more calves, and the ground crew slaps on brands and ear marks and performs quick medical operations to turn bulls into steers.

Badger is new, so his job is to be a mugger and wrestle calves to the ground. Experienced muggers work effortlessly, oftentimes using just one hand apiece as they team up to drop the calf and hold it securely.

But Badger's timing is off, pulling a little early or a little late. And the young cowboy still hasn't figured out whether he should pull the rope or the calf's tail, and it is seemingly different for every calf. Out of sync, Badger and the man opposite look like they are riding a teeter-totter, tugging back and forth.

I've driven a stagecoach, helped build a dam, and beat a gang of cattle rustlers, Badger thinks. *Surely I can figure this out.*

Badger's fellow mugger yells, "Together now," and they pull in opposite directions at the same time.

As Badger holds his first calf in place, dust swirls in every direction. The branding iron is applied, and the thick smoke seems to go everywhere but up. As the smoke plays ring-around-the-rosy in Badger's face, he can hardly breathe. It chokes his lungs, burns his nose, and irritates his eyes. The smell of burning hair is nothing like wood smoke. It smells worse than the cheapest tobacco. The unique odor can only be described as the smell of branding.

Despite all the drawbacks, Badger is surprised at how fun branding is. All the cowboys talk and tell jokes. A few play practical jokes on the others. And the work gets easier the more Badger does it.

It takes about a half hour to brand sixteen calves with the neighbors' irons. Charlie pulls out the biggest ones to correct the misbranded calves even though he is certain that someone else misbranded them. After that, they only use the Shoesole brand.

With the work all done, Charlie, Badger, and Gib herd the cattle through the gateway and toward a small pasture, where the cowboys will store the cattle for a couple days so they can help with the rest of the rodeo before driving their herd back to their ranch.

THE SHADOWS ARE CREEPING out as Charlie, Badger, and Gib move the herd. Gib is out at point, and Charlie and Badger push the drag.

"There's a lot about brandin' I haven't figured out," Badger says to Charlie as they stroll lazily behind the herd.

"How's that?" Charlie responds.

"So, why do you have a brand … and an ear mark … and a waddle?" Badger asks.

"Well, Badger, we wanna be sure we get all our cows back," Charlie says. "So the more ways we have to identify 'em, the better. I can spot a Shoesole cow if I see her brand, but I can also spot her if I see her left ear or her right hip. It's the same for all the neighbors too. A rafter-S is always a Strickland cow. Mr. Winters has the FW brand. Mrs. Salles' cows all have a 7Z, and Mr. Caudle uses CC."

"What about the brandin' iron?" Badger asks. "It looks like it hurts."

"It does," Charlie says. "Don't touch a hot iron. It hurts real bad."

"I mean for the calves," Badger explains. "Don't you think it hurts 'em?"

"Well, I asked a calf once if it hurt."

"You did?" Badger asks with his head tilted and eyebrows raised. "What did it say?"

"Mooooo!" Charlie cries out.

Badger grins and then laughs.

"Mooooo," Charlie says again.

"So what does that mean in English?"

"Owwwww!" Charlie cries.

Badger laughs again.

"So the calf squirms and is uncomfortable, but it always jumps up and runs back to its cow," Charlie explains.

"I know we brand to identify whose cow is whose," Badger says, "but is it really the best way?"

"Well, cows can't talk and say who they belong to," Charlie says. "Even if they could, I know cows well enough that I wouldn't trust 'em. It would be nice if everyone's cows would just come home in the fall. But if they were smart enough to do that, we'd be outta jobs."

Badger smiles like a court jester as Charlie's plain-spoken logic sinks in.

Meanwhile, Gib has the herd leaders moving past a wooden gate into a wide meadow. A rock rim surrounds most of the pasture with a barbed wire fence across the bottom and a man-made rock fence to close the gaps in the rim rock.

Gib rides back to the drag. "We've got a problem, Charlie."

"We usually do, Gib," Charlie replies. "Good thing we get paid to fix problems."

Gib grins. "All five wires on the fence are cut, and boot prints are all around the area."

"I bet I know who did it," Badger says. "Those Joiner brothers are doin' everythin' they can to get us to leave."

"I have a suspicion they aren't workin' alone," Charlie says. "I'd bet somebody is pullin' their strings, someone who's payin' 'em to do it."

"Who?" Badger asks.

"That's a good question," Charlie replies. "If y'all figure that out, then ya will have fixed our biggest problem."

Chapter 5

BEEF AND POTATOES BOIL in the stewpot. With the rodeo done for the day, most of the ranchers and ranch hands mill about the wagons. They talk, laugh, and joke with one another as Badger watches from the edge of the crowd. With such a large number of people to feed every night, it makes sense to eat fresh beef. Not rabbit or venison, not sage chicken or jerky, but fresh cooked beef.

Beef, beef, beef, beef, is Badger's top thought. *The best part of the rodeo is the food.*

Badger fills a plate and sits alone. He takes his first bite, and his eyes close in bliss as he savors the chunks of meat and bland potatoes. Someone approaches. Badger looks up just in time to see a booted foot tip Badger's plate in his lap.

Hank Joiner grins at Badger like a dog who's having his belly scratched. Badger picks a chunk of meat from his lap and places it in his mouth. Then he stands up. He glares into Hank's eyes and says, "I know what you're doin' here, Hank, and I don't like it."

"We want you gone," Hank replies.

"We?" Badger asks. "Do you have a mouse in your pocket? So you and your halfwit brother want us gone, but everybody else here doesn't mind us bein' here. They all like us."

"Fred Winters wants you gone," Hank says, his hands on his hips, leaning in toward Badger. He suddenly winces, realizing Badger has outwitted him. "Um, er, Mr. Strickland doesn't want you here, and Mr. Caudle hates everyone."

Badger chuckles as he watches Hank squirm. Hank's eyes narrow, and he slugs Badger in the gut. Badger's swelling pride pops like a balloon, and the young cowboy falls to the ground, holding his middle. The Joiner brother stalks away.

Badger gasps as he tries to catch his breath and keep his two bites of dinner from coming back up.

I have to find Charlie.

Badger knows where to look. A brush-free flat sits just past the wagons. Charlie usually hangs out there. Badger lurches to a stand, rubs his stomach, and slumps toward Charlie.

Charlie and a small group of boys all have ropes out and are roping a large wooden log standing on end. Charlie is coaching the boys. He gives them roping tips and little adjustments with every loop they throw.

Charlie spots Badger. "Hey, cowboy, are ya savin' some of yer stew for later?" Charlie asks as he points to Badger's shirt and pants.

"No, Charlie. I had a conversation with Hank, and he tipped over my plate and slugged me in the stomach," Badger says.

"Y'all need to find some better dinner conversation," Charlie jokes.

Badger laughs and then thinks, *Maybe Charlie isn't jokin'. I really should find some better dinner conversation.*

"I found out who the Joiner brothers are workin' for," Badger says.

"Who's that, Badger?"

"Mr. Winters," Badger says proudly.

"Do ya know why?" Charlie asks.

Badger groans. He got slugged in the stomach to get this bit of information.

"Why do we need to know a motive?" Badger asks.

"If I'm gonna stand up to a man and accuse him of somethin', I need evidence. I need to understand his motive," Charlie says, "and I need a remedy to get him to stop."

"I'll keep tryin' to get information. Hank and Harlan Joiner really like to bully me," Badger says.

"Well, y'all need to stand up to 'em," Charlie says. "Bullies are just loud cowards."

"There's two of 'em," Badger complains. "If I stand up to Hank, his brother is always lurkin' nearby waitin' to jump in and gang up on me."

"Then don't stand up to 'em alone," Charlie says.

"But you were back here, and Gib was over with the horses," Badger explains.

"And me and Gib are the only ones here?" Charlie asks. "There's almost fifty people over there, and y'all were eatin' alone. Most of 'em are friendly if ya give 'em a chance."

"I'll give 'em a chance," Badger says, "and I'll keep lookin' for answers."

Badger turns to go but stops short. "Charlie, do you know why Mr. Winters wants us outta here?"

"I have my suspicions," Charlie says. "I would guess Mr. Winters wants more grass for his cows. And if we pull our cows out, then Mr. Winters would have that. But I guess there's somethin' more. Whenever people like Mr. Winters get around me, it's usually somethin' more."

Badger sees the customary smile drain off Charlie's face. He wants to ask about that "somethin' more," but Charlie's new expression keeps him quiet.

THE SUN IS COMPLETELY down, and darkness covers most of the desert. A campfire burns brightly in the middle of camp, and everyone gathers around the warmth and light. The second day of the rodeo is winding down.

A small band plays fiddle, guitar, and spoons. Gib joins in on the harmonica. It's a lively tune. Children dance around the fire. A few people clap along with the music, which is out of time and a little out of tune. But this is the best band in the neighborhood, so everyone listens.

Badger sits alone like a Hereford bull in the wintertime until Charlie's words play through his head. So Badger walks over and sits next to Mr. Caudle. The rancher looks to Badger and nods. Badger shoots a toothless smile back.

"Nice evenin' we're havin'," Badger says as friendly as he can.

Mr. Caudle nods in agreement and then nods toward the full moon.

"Yeah, it is nice havin' a full moon," Badger says. "I don't like it much when it gets completely dark."

Mr. Caudle nods. The quiet cowboy looks drab. His hat is old and tattered and has a black sweat ring around the base of the crown. His faded, dusty pants were once blue. He wears a faded blue shirt and a faded gray scarf. He doesn't wear any jewelry or have fringe on anything, unlike other cowboys in the rodeo. His mouth frowns, but his eyes dance with gentle happiness.

I'm terrible at makin' conversation—and new friends, Badger thinks. Suffocating on the awkward silence, Badger squirms and searches his brain for something else to say.

"Did you get your cows over to your place all right?" Badger asks.

Mr. Caudle nods.

Badger grimaces. He doesn't know what else to say.

Mr. Caudle notices Badger's distress, so he nods toward the band.

"Do you like the band?" Badger blurts out like a guilty bank robber confessing a crime. "I like the band."

Mr. Caudle points to his ear and then points to the band.

"We should enjoy the music as long as it plays?" Badger asks.

Mr. Caudle taps Badger's knee and nods.

Badger sits quietly and listens to the music. Instead of being uncomfortable, Badger enjoys the makeshift band and Mr. Caudle's company. A few people dance like a lek of strutting sage roosters. A few more clap with the music, but most have no outward expression. One by one, the audience leaves until about a half dozen people are left listening to the band play one last ballad. The last note from the fiddle echoes into the evening, and Gib slides the harmonica back into his pocket. The spoons player returns the spoons to the buckaroo wagon.

Badger looks over to Mr. Caudle and says with a grin, "I enjoyed sittin' with you tonight."

Mr. Caudle nods in agreement and pats Badger on the shoulder. Badger takes this to mean Mr. Caudle enjoyed the evening also.

"I'll see you in the mornin'," Badger says, turning to leave. "Oh, one more question. Do you know why Mr. Winters hates us at the Shoesole so much?"

Mr. Caudle nods.

"Why?" Badger asks.

Mr. Caudle points at Badger and shakes his head no. Then he points to Gib and Charlie and shakes his head no.

Badger thinks for a moment and then says. "Is it somethin' against Colonel McGill?"

Mr. Caudle nods.

"What does Mr. Winters have against Colonel McGill?" Badger asks.

Mr. Caudle reaches into his pocket and pulls out two shiny quarters. He holds them up and rubs the silver coins together between his thumb and forefinger.

"It's about money?" Badger asks.

Mr. Caudle shakes his head no and emphatically holds the coins up again.

Badger thinks carefully. "It's about silver?"

Mr. Caudle nods. He shakes the silver and drops the coins in his pocket.

"So it's about silver," Badger says, pretending he understands. "Thanks for your help."

Mr. Caudle nods and turns to leave.

"Good night," Badger says.

Mr. Caudle waves without turning around.

THE MORNING AIR IS brisk, not cold but definitely chilly. The third day at the rodeo is a little bit easier. The bumps and bruises from the previous two days' mishaps are still painful but more manageable, and most of Badger's muscles are stretched out. Badger reluctantly squirms out of his bedroll and into his clothes and coat.

Charlie pours a cup of coffee and hands it to Badger, and the sleepy teen warms his hands on the sides of the cup.

"Mornin', Badger," Charlie says with a smile.

"Mornin'," Badger replies much less enthusiastically.

"Did ya enjoy the dance last night?" Charlie asks.

"I save all my dances for Nettie McCorkle," Badger replies. "So I only listened last night."

"This Nettie McCorkle, y'all dance with her at other dances?" Charlie asks, looking at Badger as suspiciously as a detective.

"I guess that's why I never dance," Badger says with a half smile. "I spent most of the night with Mr. Caudle."

"There's none better than Mr. Caudle," Charlie says around a sip of coffee. "Ask anybody here."

Badger tilts his head and furrows his brow. "I don't understand why everyone likes him so much. I spent a couple hours with him and had to carry the conversation. Have you ever tried to have a conversation with someone who doesn't talk?"

"I talk with Mr. Caudle all the time," Charlie says before spitting out some coffee grounds. "I always enjoy our talks. And I'm not alone. I've never heard anybody say a cross word 'bout Mr. Caudle, well, except y'all, Badger."

"I just don't get it." Badger breaks off a stale piece of biscuit and drops it in his mouth. "Everyone likes him, but nobody has ever heard him say a word."

"Maybe that's it, Badger," Charlie says.

"Whattaya mean?" Badger asks as the stale biscuit swirls around his tongue.

"Well, I've had people dislike me because of somethin' I've said," Charlie says. "Usually somethin' stupid or mean or hurtful. But I've never made someone mad from somethin' I didn't say."

"You might be on to somethin'," Badger says.

"I'm sure I am," Charlie says. "Maybe I should keep my mouth shut more."

"But he did give me a clue about Mr. Winters," Badger says.

"If he didn't say anythin', how did ya pick up a clue?"

"When I asked him, he pulled out two silver quarters and rubbed 'em together."

"It's 'bout money?" Charlie guesses.

"That was my first guess too, but Mr. Caudle said no. He said it was about silver."

"'Bout silver?" Charlie's eyes light up, and his head jerks back with surprise.

"You know what he means?" Badger asks.

"I think I do," Charlie says. "It might be 'bout politics."

"Politics?"

"Yeah. Colonel McGill is a member of the Silver Party," Charlie says. "He's thinkin' 'bout runnin' for county commissioner. And if Mr. Winters is in the Democratic Party, then I'm almost sure it's 'bout politics."

"You really think a political feud could lead to Mr. Winters hirin' the Joiner brothers to get rid of us?" Badger asks.

"Well, a few years ago, the governor was killed over politics," Charlie says. "And 'bout a decade ago, I had a friend get into a gunfight at a political meetin'."

Killin' over politics? Badger shakes his head. *I thought politics was just made up to sell newspapers.*

"So what do we do about it?" Badger asks.

"Well, right now we have cows to gather," Charlie says.

"I mean after that," Badger says.

"We do what ya should always do with a bully," Charlie says. "We stand up to 'em."

"Which one?" Badger asks. "The Joiner brothers or Mr. Winters?"

"All three," Charlie says, "or whoever is doin' the bullyin'. But, Badger, don't stand up to 'em alone."

"I know," Badger says. "I'm makin' friends. I guess the more I have, the better off I'll be."

Chapter 6

THE HERD IS GATHERED, and six cowboys, including Badger, hold the cattle next to the fence. Mr. Strickland and Mr. Caudle sort cows and calves with a rafter-S brand out of the herd. On the south end of the herd, cowboys weave back and forth on their horses. One cow tries to leave, so a cowboy runs her down and turns her back to the herd. The horses sweat, and the riders move constantly.

Badger is on the north end of the herd. About every ten minutes, a cow or calf tries to walk away, so Badger has to turn it around. That means Badger has to pay attention, which makes the job even more boring. It is so boring, in fact, that Badger makes a list in his head of tasks that would be just as boring as holding herd.

Watchin' grass grow ... watchin' paint dry ... shuckin' peas ... farmin', Badger thinks. *Goin' to a tea party ... English class at school.*

As Badger's mind wanders, he loses track of where everything is. He notices a calf leaving the herd, so he pushes him back. Then Badger contemplates some of the philosophical challenges of his time.

Why do we study math and English but never use it? Why is there pain and sufferin' in the world? Why are girls so complicated?

Badger looks up and flinches. Mr. Caudle and his horse are standing right in front of him.

Mr. Caudle whirls his hand in a circle, waving for Badger to follow him. Badger cautiously follows, but Mr. Caudle moves again and then points right behind his horse's tail.

Badger gently spurs Blue, and catches up to Mr. Caudle's horse. The older cowboy rides with elegance, as though he and his horse were one. Mr. Caudle is as comfortable around horses and cattle as he is awkward around people.

Mr. Caudle rides lazily into the herd with Badger and Blue tucked neatly behind him like a foal following a mare.

As they ride through the herd, Mr. Caudle's head swivels left and right. He surveys all the cows, looking for a rafter-S brand. Mr. Caudle points to a cow with a rafter-S prominently displayed on her side. He falls in behind the cow, and the cow moves to the south. Her calf follows dutifully beside her just like Badger follows dutifully behind Mr. Caudle.

Badger isn't sure, but he thinks Mr. Caudle is teaching him how to sort out a cow. Mr. Caudle is a

perfect teacher, because the skill of sorting a cow is difficult to explain but fairly simple to show.

As the cow reaches the edge of the herd, she balks. The calf wanders away from her side, and they refuse to exit. Mr. Caudle gently moves his horse to the left, the calf moves back to the right, and the cow and calf cautiously move forward again. Badger mirrors Mr. Caudle as best he can.

The cow looks left and then right, wanting to escape back into the herd. But Mr. Caudle is everywhere she looks. She steps out of the herd and bends back to the right. With very slight movements, Mr. Caudle cuts her off. At about ten yards out of the herd, the cow gives up and walks away from Mr. Caudle. After another ten paces, she sees the smaller herd and eagerly joins it.

Mr. Caudle nods at Badger and then turns back into the herd. They sort out several more pairs. Mr. Caudle moves slowly and makes very subtle changes in direction. Badger tries to copy Mr. Caudle.

Blue is as clumsy as Badger as they walk a little bit past where they need to or stop a little bit short. Badger's jerky movements stir the herd a little, but he's figuring it out.

Mr. Caudle points to the next pair. The cow is old and the calf is young, so they should be easy to sort. He looks back at Badger and motions for him to sort them out of the herd.

Badger gulps.

The young cowboy takes a deep breath and straightens his reins. Badger walks Blue toward the cow, and she instinctively moves. Badger and the cow and calf walk to the edge of the herd. The cow is surprisingly cooperative.

Badger gets to the edge, and the cow and calf slide out of the herd. The pair join the smaller herd. Badger turns back to the bigger herd and realizes Mr. Caudle has been helping him from behind.

This isn't as hard as it looks, Badger thinks. *Especially with Mr. Caudle backin' me up.*

Badger grins at Mr. Caudle. Mr. Caudle smiles back and gives Badger a thumbs up.

As Mr. Caudle rides back into the herd, Badger sees a horse and rider cresting the horizon at a dead run. It's like a single-horse stampede.

Badger's jaw drops as he stares.

The horse runs to within three hundred yards of Badger and bucks. It's a long-stride buck, so not very powerful. But the horse and rider still cover a lot of ground quickly.

Charlie pulls his rope from beside his saddle horn and spurs his horse toward the incoming rider.

Badger squints his eyes and makes out Hank Joiner astride the runaway bronc.

Charlie builds a loop with his rope as he rides at a full gallop. He swings wide from the oncoming horse and then rounds back next to the horse and rider.

As they approach the herd, Charlie swings his loop twice and throws the rope. The lariat twists and unfolds as it swirls gracefully through the air. The rope hits the horse on the back of the neck and the loop settles over the horse's head. Charlie pulls the slack, and the rope tightens around the horse's neck. Charlie swings the tail end of the rope around his saddle horn, which slows and then stops Hank's horse.

The winded horse gasps for air as he stands at the end of the rope. Charlie slacks the rope and rides closer to Hank.

"How dare you rope my horse!" Hank yells.

"I wasn't tryin' to help ya, believe me," Charlie replies. "But I didn't want y'all and yer horse to fly into here and scatter the herd."

"Maybe I was tryin' to scatter the herd," Hank spits.

"That's even more reason to stop ya," Charlie says.

"Why don't you catch a clue?" Hank sneers. "We don't want you here."

"I've got work to do here," Charlie says. "As long as Colonel McGill wants us here, we'll be here."

"We'll see about that."

Hank yanks the rope off his horse. He pulls the beast back to the south. He passes three other herd holders and rides up to Badger.

"Howdy, Hank," Badger sneers, pretending to be friendly. "Lovely mornin' for a horseback ride."

Hank rides closer to Badger. He doesn't say a word; his evil grin just gets wider and wider with every step. Badger braces himself. Blue becomes equally skittish as Hank and his bronc close the gap.

Hank pulls right next to Badger and sits silently for longer than the teen is comfortable. In a move Badger has seen before, Hank reaches out to pull Badger from the saddle.

But this time, Blue jumps to the left, and Badger holds tightly to the saddle horn. Hank's bronc jumps to the right. Hank flops to the ground, and his ride runs wildly over the same horizon Blue ran over a couple days earlier. Badger pulls Blue around and quickly regains control. Hank struggles to catch his breath.

Charlie rides over and grins at Badger.

"Whattaya say, Badger? Do y'all think it's yer turn to ride? Fetchin' Hank's horse will give him a chance to catch his breath, get angry, pitch a fit, and cool down again before ya get back."

Badger nods, a twinkle in his eye, and he and Blue ride off toward the horizon to retrieve Hank's wayward pony.

LUNCH IS ALWAYS BRIEF. Some days the cowboys don't even come to the wagons; they just eat jerky and biscuits, or hardtack. But today the sorting goes smoothly, and they finish just as the sun is at its highest point.

Lunch at the wagons is still fairly simple. The cowboys dine on fresh biscuits and beef steaks. Sliced thin, the steaks cook fast. With the sun beating down, no one except the cook lingers near the fire.

Badger, Gib, and Charlie sit in a semicircle and quickly eat their small meal. They eat in silence—well, not silence, because they chew and slurp and snort like a litter of piglets. Once the food is gone, they relax with their warm coffee and chat.

"So, Badger, how did ya like wranglin' Hank's horse for him?" Charlie asks, struggling to hold back a laugh.

"I didn't really like it, but it was better than standin' around like a fool who's waitin' for his horse to come back," Badger says.

"Did ya stand up to him?" Charlie asks.

"I didn't have to," Badger says. "He tried to bully me but fell off his horse instead."

"I'm gettin' a little worried about the Joiner brothers," Gib says around the stem of grass between his lips.

"Why's that, Gib?" Charlie asks, leaning forward.

"Well, it seems like they're runnin' outta ideas," Gib says. "They still want us gone, but their tricks aren't workin'."

"Do you think they'll give up?" Badger asks.

"I'm guessin' not," Charlie says and then sips his coffee. He swallows. "If they can't get rid of us, I doubt they get paid."

"Whattaya think they'll do next?" Badger asks.

"I think Gib's right. I think they're outta ideas," Charlie says. "So I'd guess ya will see more of the same but worse."

"Worse?" Badger asks.

"Yeah, worse. I bet they'll just kick it up a notch and be nastier."

"How do we stop 'em?"

"The only way we can," Charlie says. "We have to stand up to 'em."

"You think we should pick a fight with the Joiner brothers?" Badger asks.

"That's not what I'm sayin' at all," Charlie says. "There's a lot of ways to stop a bully. Bein' a bully back isn't the best way."

"So how do I stand up without fightin' back?" Badger asks, tipping his hat back and scratching his head.

"Badger, have ya seen somebody get mad and punch a wall?" Charlie asks.

"I saw my friend Percy do that one time. He missed the wood wall and hit the bricks. I think he broke his pinky finger," Badger says with a chuckle.

"Have ya ever seen the wall fight back?"

"No."

"Have ya ever seen the wall crumble?"

"No," Badger says. "I usually see the chump try to shake the pain outta his hand."

"The chump usually gives up after one punch," Charlie punches at the air to make his point. "Y'all need to be like that wall. Stand up to 'em. Don't back down. Don't crumble, and they'll back down. They just might respect ya after."

"I'd plan on standin' up to 'em, Badger," Gib says. "'Cause we aren't goin' anywhere, and they aren't goin' anywhere."

Charlie sips his coffee and then dumps the last swallow on the ground.

"Enough lazin' around," Charlie says. "Let's rodeo."

Gib and Badger dump their coffee grounds on the dirt and jump to their feet. Badger rubs his stomach and belches as the coffee, steak, and biscuits churn in his belly. Badger has learned not to overeat at lunch, because it's hard to work with a full stomach.

Badger smiles as he watches Charlie mount up and ride away. *He really loves what he's doin',* Badger thinks. *So do I—most of the time.*

Badger shares part of a biscuit with Blue, and Blue nuzzles Badger's shoulder. He swings onto Blue and rides back to work.

Chapter 7

DUST IS EVERYWHERE. It sticks to every stitch of clothing Badger wears. His gray hat is turning brown, and the dust mixes with sweat to cake onto his face and neck. Flies and gnats buzz around all the humans and beasts. The latter swish their tails to send the pests away.

That is actually all Badger sees—swaying cow tails lined out in front of him like a marina of sailboats tied up in a tempest.

Most of the cows know where they're supposed to go. Most calves don't, but they follow their mothers. Badger's job is to herd any lost cows and calves. Some cows are just stubborn. Some cows are certain they've left their calves behind. All the calves that can't find their mothers run in search of them. But Badger persistently pushes them along.

The young cowboy is "pushing up." Badger will spend the afternoon moving this bunch of cows closer to the rodeo grounds to speed the morning's gather up.

The teen settles into the monotony.

His heart suddenly jumps when he sees a cowboy riding his way. *A Joiner brother and I'm all alone!*

Badger squints to bring the rider into focus.

Wait. Is that Percy Reed? Badger wonders. Badger leaves his post and spurs Blue toward the rider.

"Howdy, Badger," Percy says.

Percy rides a big gray horse. He tries hard to look like a cowboy and has the money for a brand-new outfit— new blue shirt, new pants, new chaps, new gloves, new brown boots, and a shiny new brown hat. With his fancy new getup, he looks more like a gambler or a government man than a cowboy.

"Hey, Percy," Badger replies. "Whatcha doin' clear over here?"

"Remember the steers I bought last winter and how they were always walkin' away?" Percy asks.

"Of course I do," Badger says. "I spent three months helpin' you round 'em up."

"Oh, yeah," Percy replies. "I still owe you two weeks' pay, don't I?"

"Don't worry about it," Badger says. "I wasn't in it for the money; I was just tryin' to be a good friend."

"Then why did you leave?" Percy asks.

Because you didn't pay me, Badger thinks. Borrowing from Mr. Caudle's act, Badger just nods his head and stays quiet. He needs friends and doesn't want to start a fight with his longest one.

"Well, my wanderin' steers broke out again," Percy says. "I figure they wandered over here and I might find 'em at the rodeo."

The two friends ride to the back of the herd and move the cows and calves forward again. They whoop and holler and ride from edge to edge like coyotes stalking prey. As Badger and Percy ride near one another, their conversation continues.

"You're ridin' with the Shoesole Ranch, aren't you?" Percy asks.

"I am," Badger says. They move apart to turn the edges of the herd and then move back together.

"I've got some bad news for you then," Percy says.

Badger isn't surprised, but he stops his horse and asks, "What's that?"

"I stopped by my dad's store on the way over here," Percy says, "and a hired gun was there buyin' supplies."

"Why's that bad news?" Badger asks.

"Well, I overheard that he'd been hired to get rid of the Shoesole Ranch boys."

"Who's this hired gun?" Badger asks.

"Sausage Pickle," Percy says.

"That's his name or what he eats for breakfast?" Badger asks.

"Breakfast?" Percy says. "That's the weirdest breakfast I've heard of. No, Badger, that's his name—Sausage Pickle."

"I'm pretty sure he's gonna shoot me," Badger says with a resigned sigh like someone just walked over his grave.

"Don't say that, Badger," Percy replies.

"It's true. 'Cause when he introduces himself as 'Sausage Pickle,' I'm gonna laugh in his face," Badger blurts with a snort. Percy laughs.

"Sausage Pickle," Badger shouts with a laugh. Percy roars with laughter.

"What kind of name is Sausage Pickle?" Badger asks again, wiping a tear from his eye.

"I think it's Italian," Percy says between laughs. "And his name might sound funny, but this gunfighter looks like he means business. You remember that steer I rode that knocked my tooth sideways?"

"Yeah. Does the tooth still wiggle?"

"A little. Anyway, he looks kind of like him. Really big and strong and kind of ugly in a fancy sort of way."

"Well, I'm not alone here, Percy," Badger says. "Besides, I have enough to worry about with the Joiner brothers."

"I know the Joiner brothers. They moved in here a few months ago, about the same time as Mr. Winters. They have a debt at my dad's store about two pages long," Percy says. "Are they givin' you a hard time?"

"Yeah. I've gotten crosswise with 'em a few times," Badger says, "especially with Hank. He's plain mean, and I think Mr. Winters is payin' 'em to get rid of us."

"Sounds like you need to stand up to him," Percy says.

"I will," Badger says, "next time I see him. In the meantime, we better get these cows movin' so we can warn Charlie and Gib."

THE SUN HANGS LOW in the western sky. Badger and Percy leave the cattle next to a small pond and ride along a trail winding through sagebrush and around rocks. About a mile from the rodeo grounds, they see Charlie and Gib riding in the same direction just east of them. Badger and Percy spur their horses into a jog to catch up with the older cowboys.

Charlie waves.

"Howdy, Charlie."

"Howdy," Charlie says. "What's the good word, Badger?"

"All I've got is bad news," Badger says.

"Oh, it can't be that bad," Charlie drawls. "Tell me somethin' good first to soften the blow."

"Uh, well, I ran into my friend Percy," Badger says.

"I see that. How y'all doin', Percy?" Charlie asks. "Has yer dad gotten in those beans and sugar I ordered last week?"

"Good to see you, Charlie," Percy replies. "And I didn't stop long enough to find out."

Percy looks at Badger's surprised face. "I've known Charlie for a while."

"Are you ready for the bad news?" Badger asks.

"Not yet," Charlie seems to be playing with Badger. "Tell me 'bout the cows."

"We got a pretty big bunch," Badger draws short. "Don't you want to know about the hired gun?"

Charlie's smile withers. He turns as serious as a student on report card day and looks straight at Badger. "Tell me 'bout the hired gun."

"Percy told me a guy has been hired to get rid of all the Shoesole Ranch cowboys," Badger says as quickly as his words will come.

"Y'all mean the Joiner brothers?" Charlie asks.

"No," Badger replies. "Sausage Pickle."

"Come again?" Charlie says with a puzzled look.

"Sausage Pickle," Badger says.

"I don't care what ya want for dinner, Badger," Charlie says. "Who's the gunman who's comin' after us?"

"His name is Sausage Pickle," Badger says.

Charlie chuckles. "Sausage Pickle? I don't think I wanna be shot by a man named Sausage Pickle."

"Well, I don't wanna be shot by anybody," Badger replies.

A long pause follows as the cowboys let the news of being hunted sink in.

"We're not leavin', are we?" Gib asks.

"I'm not leavin'," Charlie says. "Colonel McGill placed a lot of trust in me to graze his cows in this area. I have a responsibility to stick around and do my job. But y'all should leave. I don't want anybody gettin' hurt over a bunch of cows."

"I'm not leavin'," Gib says. "I work for the colonel, same as you."

Badger hesitates. He wants to help, but he doesn't want Sausage Pickle to shoot him. Badger is really getting tired of bullies.

"You told me I need to stand up to bullies," Badger says. "I still need to stand up to the Joiner brothers. If I survive that, I might as well stick around and stand up to Sausage Pickle too."

"Well, y'all should get a chance pretty quick here," Charlie says.

"Whattaya mean?" Badger asks.

"Here come the Joiner brothers, and Hank looks like he's got half a mad on," Charlie says. "Here's yer chance to stand up to him."

BADGER DISMOUNTS AND SWIRLS his hobbles around Blue's hooves. Charlie, Gib, and Percy stay mounted and stand behind Badger. With the hobbles, Blue can't stray very far or leave very fast. Badger looks down and takes two deep breaths.

Hank and Harlan casually ride up to Badger, and Hank swings off his horse. Hank, wearing his evil grin, moves to within reach of Badger, and Badger steps back.

You need to stand up to him, Badger tells himself.

Badger quickly rebounds and steps back to Hank. Badger's step forward is bigger than his step back. Badger is surprised to be standing eye to eye, nose to nose, and chin to chin with Hank.

Hank recoils like a baby sucking on a lemon, but he doesn't step back.

"Whatcha doin'?" Hank asks.

"I'm tired of you and your brother pushin' me around," Badger says louder than necessary. He glares into Hank's yellow eyes.

Hank sneers and pulls back slightly. "I'm done pushin' you around, Badger."

Surprise washes away Badger's scowl.

"You're done pushin' me around?"

"There's no money in it," Hank shrugs.

"You mean you were bullyin' me just for money?" Badger asks.

78

"Not just for money," Hank says. "It's kind of fun pickin' on you."

"Well, who was payin' you?" Badger asks, already knowing the answer.

"Mr. Winters," Hank said. "But he got annoyed that we couldn't scare even you off. So he hired some enforcer from down at the mines—some Italian gunslinger."

"Sausage Pickle?" Badger asks.

"Yeah, somethin' like that," Hank says.

"Why does Mr. Winters want us outta here?" Badger asks.

"I don't know," Hank says. "When somebody offers you money for an easy job, you don't ask too many questions."

"So just like that, you're givin' up?"

"There's no money in it, and if you're gonna stand up for yourself, there's no fun in it either," Hank says, taking a step back.

"So you really don't know why Mr. Winters wants us gone?" Badger digs one more time.

"Don't overthink it, Badger. This Sausage Pickle or whatever his name is doesn't work for cheap. It's pretty plain Mr. Winters wants the Shoesole cowboys off this range bad."

"Thanks for the warnin' about the gunslinger," Badger says.

"I'm not tryin' to help you," Hank says, looking at Badger like he recently stepped in a cow pie. "I'm mad I'm not gettin' paid. Nothin' would make me happier than if you'd leave so there's no bounty for this Italian."

"Well, we aren't gonna run or be bullied." Badger steps toward Hank and glares into his eyes.

"Don't bring it up with me," Hank says, swinging up onto his horse. "Take it up with the quick-shootin' gunslinger."

Badger exhales. Standing up to Hank had been easy—too easy. Standing up to a hired gun would be difficult—maybe even deadly.

THE CAMPFIRE GLOWS UNDER the dark night sky. About fifteen cowboys crowd around the boiling coffee pot. Each man warms his hands around a steaming tin cup of thick black liquid. The glow under their hats and the steam rising in front of their faces make all the cowboys look like gargoyles on a foggy night.

The men chatter idly like the banter at a barber shop until the fire dies down. It's as if everyone runs out of things to talk about at the same time, and they turn their attention to Mr. Strickland.

The rancher notices, so he speaks for the group. "Everyone has heard about this Sausage Pickle comin' for you, Charlie." Mr. Strickland pauses and most everyone nods in agreement. "Whatcha gonna do?"

"I don't know that there is anythin' to do," Charlie replies. "We have two, maybe three more days here at the rodeo. After that, we all go our separate ways."

"You're not worried?" Mr. Strickland asks.

"Worried?" Charlie asks. "Just the mention of his name makes me hungry."

Everyone laughs uncomfortably.

"I can't help but be a little bit worried—more for my crew and my cows than for me. But I've got a job to do, and I aim to finish it."

"Are you gonna have to stand up to him?" Badger asks.

"I'm not gonna wander outta my way to get into a confrontation with this fella. But if it comes to it, I won't back down."

"You won't be standin' by yourself," Gib says stoutly. "I'll stand with you."

"So will I," Badger adds.

"Me too."

"Same here."

"I'll stand with you."

"Well, there all y'all have it," Charlie says. "It'll be a whole lot easier to stand up to this Sausage Pickle if we all stand together."

"I'd like to know how you plan on standin' up to Sausage Pickle," Mr. Strickland says. "I've never seen you carry a pistol. Are you plannin' on fightin' back?"

"I don't know much. But I do know that bullyin' a bully makes ya nothin' better than a bully."

"But this guy sounds like a killer."

"Then I guess we'll just have to stand strong," Charlie says matter-of-factly.

The men swirl the coffee grounds in the bottom of their mugs. Badger hears a coyote howling in the distance. He turns to Percy who looks about as sick as Badger feels.

"Hey, Percy, you remember the time you tricked me into drinkin' the tobacco spit can at your dad's store?" he asks quietly.

"Heh. Yeah, I remember. You kind of turned white, then green and your lips turned blue," Percy says. "What about it?"

"That's the kind of sick I feel right now," Badger whispers. "How can Charlie stand up to a gunslinger without usin' a gun?"

"I don't know, Badger," Percy whispers grimly.

It's as if the fire knows the meeting is over, because the flame flickers its last light. Darkness closes in around the glowing embers, and a thin stream of smoke climbs into the night.

Charlie is first to pour his last three sips of coffee on the fire. Gib and Mr. Strickland follow. Badger has about half a cup left, so he slurps down a few more gulps, makes a disgusted face, and then pours his last three sips on the fire. By the time everyone has dumped the last of their coffee on the coals, only steam, smoke, and darkness remain.

The exhausted cowboys quietly roll out their bedrolls and prepare to sleep. Everyone sleeps soundly because they're exhausted. If they weren't so tired, they would be tossing and turning thinking about the dreaded gunfighter Sausage Pickle.

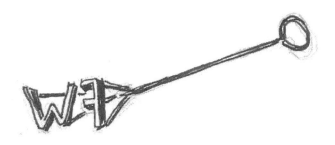

Chapter 8

SAUSAGE PICKLE. BADGER'S FIRST thought this morning is unpleasant. *Sausage Pickle will surely arrive today. Just thinkin' about Sausage Pickle makes me hungry.*

His mouth waters as he catches a whiff of breakfast cooking near the buckaroo wagons. It's fresh beef steaks with biscuits and gravy. The smell is enough to get Badger moving.

The morning is dull and gray as the sun struggles to peek over the eastern mountains. A few rattles and clanks come from the cooks at work, and a couple cows moo in the distance.

Badger pulls on his blue britches and slides into his red plaid shirt. There's just a nip of cold in the air, so Badger works quickly. He wraps his scarf around his neck and ties two quick knots to secure it. He swims into his leather vest and pulls his boots onto his feet. He flops his hat on his head and walks to the campfire.

Gib is wrangling the horses, and Charlie already has a cup of coffee and is joking with the cooks. Charlie's as relaxed as a hound dog sunning himself on a warm day.

And it seems everyone except Badger is calm.

"Mornin', Badger," Percy says between slurps of coffee while lounging in his shiny boots and dapper hat.

"Mornin'," Badger says. "You sure seem relaxed. Aren't you worried about Sausage Pickle?"

"Not anymore," Percy says. "I'm not with the Shoesole Ranch. He was pretty specific about Shoesole Ranch hands."

"So you're stickin' around then?"

"I'm not very strong or intimidatin'. I don't have a pistol," Percy says. "Really, the only thing I could do is be a shield for you."

"You'd do that for me?" Badger asks, touched.

"No, I won't take a bullet for you, Badger. I learned my lesson runnin' from the law for you when you got crosswise with that gambler," Percy says as he pours out the last of his coffee and stands to leave. "I'm not gonna be here. I found my steers, so I'm headin' back to my place before they wander off again."

"It'd be nice to have you around," Badger pleads.

"I could use your help with the steers," Percy replies. "The trail leavin' here is a pretty easy one."

Badger ponders Percy's offer. *Just leave this mess behind,* Badger considers. *That would probably keep me alive longer. But Percy doesn't really need my help, and Charlie does. And Percy doesn't pay very well— sometimes not at all, and Charlie always pays right on time.*

"I'm gonna stay here," Badger says with a sigh of regret.

"Stay safe," Percy says. "I'd like to see you again one day."

"Don't start plannin' my funeral just yet," Badger says. "I'm not gonna do anythin' stupid—just stand up to a gunfighter."

"Yeah, nothin' stupid," Percy says with an eye roll as he swings onto his horse and rides away.

LIKE A MINER LIGHTING dynamite, Badger's hand shakes as he pours a cup of coffee. He's not cold enough to shiver; it might just be nerves. Badger sips the coffee. The warmth makes Badger's belly tingle as the coffee sharpens his nerves. Badger warms his hands around the cup and surveys the horizon.

Among the long shadows, Badger sees dust in the distance.

"What's kickin' up that dust?" Badger asks as he points to the eastern trail.

"Whatever it is, we'll know soon enough," Charlie says.

"Is it Sausage Pickle?" Badger asks.

"Sausage Pickle," Charlie laughs. "Who names their kid Sausage Pickle? Relax, Badger."

Badger forces a chuckle and sits down.

Charlie talks and jokes with the cooks as he downs another cup of coffee. Badger trains his gaze on the distant dust.

How could I possibly relax with a gunslinger comin'? Badger wonders.

Badger spots a lone rider on a gray horse amid the dust and points him out to Charlie.

"He'll be here soon enough, Badger," Charlie says. "Have some breakfast."

Charlie steps to the buckaroo wagon and drops two biscuits onto a plate. The cook pours steaming gravy onto the flaky biscuits. Badger follows his lead, and they both sit near the fire and shovel food into their mouths.

With breakfast distracting all the cowboys, the rider pulls into camp, dismounts, and walks to the buckaroo wagon without anyone looking up from their food.

"Mornin'," Charlie says to the stranger.

"*Buongiorno,*" the stranger replies.

Everyone flashes a quick look at the foreign words.

"Good morning," the man clarifies. "Do you have some breakfast for a stranger?" He speaks in a staccato Italian accent. His clean black hat is perfectly round and ashtrayed on top. His black pants are freshly pressed, and he wears a long black coat, a thin black bowtie, and knee-high black boots. He wears a frilly shirt and black vest with a fancy silver pattern on it. The stranger is fairly short but is as stocky as a team of oxen. He has a scar that runs from just below his eye to just above his jaw.

"Grab a plate, stranger," Charlie says without looking up. Charlie acts just like normal. But Badger is a bundle of nerves and chases his remaining biscuit around his plate with a fork.

"Are you gentlemen with the, how you say, Boot Heel Ranch?" the stranger asks.

"Do ya mean the Shoesole Ranch?" Charlie asks.

"Yes, yes," the stranger replies. "The Shoesole Ranch. Are you with the Shoesole Ranch?"

"We are," Charlie replies. For the first time, Charlie seems to tense up a little bit. "Y'all must be Sausage Pickle."

"Sausage Pickle? Why do you call me 'Sausage Pickle'?" the stranger's sing-songy voice becomes agitated. "Do you think of me as just some sour meat product stuffed into casing?"

"Now don't get angry," Charlie says. "That's the name we were told. Set me straight. What's yer name?"

"I am Sebastiano Piccolo, famous boxing star and gunfighter extraordinaire." Mr. Piccolo puffs out his chest and raises his chin as he speaks.

"You make your livin' as a gunfighter?" Badger asks.

"That is right, and I will need to know the names of everyone here," Mr. Piccolo says, pulling out a notebook and pen.

"I'm Badger Thurston," Badger says.

"Could you spell that for me?"

"B-A-D-G-E-R—T-H-U-R-S-T-O-N," Badger replies.

"Badger? You mean like a rat or a rodent? This is your name?" Mr. Piccolo asks.

"That's what everyone calls me," Badger replies.

The stranger writes in the notebook. He works his way around the buckaroo wagon, reaching first the cook, then several other cowboys. He asks Mr. Strickland his name and writes it in the book. Finally he reaches Charlie.

"What is your name, cowboy?" Mr. Piccolo asks. Badger doesn't like the way he says "cowboy" like it's a bad word.

"Charlie Pickett," Charlie says, scrunching up his nose in curiosity. The stranger writes the name in his notebook. "Now, stranger, why are ya writin' all our names down? Rumor was you're here to scare away some cowboys. Y'all are actin' like a census taker or some other government guy."

"Ha, ha," Mr. Piccolo squawks. Badger's pretty sure it's a fake laugh. If it isn't, Badger feels sorry for him. "I am a fighter, and this is a list I keep of all the men I can beat in a fight."

"I don't believe ya can beat me in a fight," Charlie says.

"Well, let me scratch your name off my list," Mr. Piccolo says. He draws a line through Charlie's name in the notebook.

"Why don't you scratch my name off your list too?" Mr. Strickland asks. The stranger dutifully scratches off the name and then puts the notebook away.

"I am not here to prove my toughness," Mr. Piccolo says. "I am here to make some money. Everyone with the Shoesole Ranch, please raise your hand. You are the only ones I need to deal with."

Charlie, Gib, and Badger raise their hands. Charlie grins, Gib looks like a brahma bull that's been cornered, and Badger is as timid as a field mouse.

"If you have to deal with the Shoesole cowboys, then you have to deal with all of us," Mr. Strickland interrupts.

The cowboys who are sitting or leaning all stand up to prove Mr. Strickland's point.

"I enjoy a good fight," Mr. Piccolo says, "but one against everyone? Well, that is not fair."

"But you'd be the one startin' it," Mr. Strickland says. "So fair or not, it would be just."

"Now, everybody, settle down," Charlie says. "Nobody needs to get hurt on my account. I'll fight ya—man to man."

"Well, that settles it then," Mr. Piccolo says. "What are your terms?"

"Loser leaves," Charlie says.

"You mean if I lose, I go back to the mines. And if you lose, you leave and take your crew with you and I get my bounty?"

"That's right," Charlie says, "and since y'all laid down the challenge, I get to choose the weapons."

"Take your pick," Mr. Piccolo says. "I can beat any man in any fight—fists, knives, guns, Japanese samurai swords, wrestl—"

"Ropes," Charlie interrupts.

"Ropes?" Mr. Piccolo asks. "Not sticks or rocks? Ropes are not weapons."

"Growin' up in the South," Charlie says, "nothin' was more frightenin' than a mob with a rope."

"You are going to hang me with a rope?" Mr. Piccolo asks.

"Of course not," Charlie says, appalled. "But y'all will know when you've been beaten."

"I would prefer a boxing match," Mr. Piccolo says. "But it is your choice, because I am a man of my word."

"I'll even let you borrow my rope," Mr. Strickland offers as he hands his coiled lariat to Mr. Piccolo.

"Don't forget yer horse," Charlie says as he points to Mr. Piccolo's mount.

"A roping contest with horses?" Mr. Piccolo asks. "Is this like jousting?"

"Call it joustin' with a rope if ya wanna," Charlie says with a smile.

"A joust. I like it," Mr. Piccolo says. "I will be ready at eight o'clock."

"Eight o'clock it is," Charlie says, "right here."

"I will be here," Mr. Piccolo says. "And I will warn you, I never lose."

Charlie nods his head and gleams a toothy grin to Mr. Piccolo and then to the other cowboys.

I don't think Mr. Piccolo knows what he's gettin' into, Badger think. *Things just might work out after all.*

IT IS THREE MINUTES until eight. The sun is high overhead, and most of the early morning shadows have shortened up. A gentle breeze stirs the dust the waiting cowboys have kicked up.

Charlie moves smoothly astride his mount, as if he were part of the horse. Charlie has a small loop built with his rope, and he spins a tight circle. The cow boss is doing tricks with his rope like he's a circus act. He pulls on the rope, and the spinning loop travels up the length of his arm and then back out like a yo-yo. He twirls the rope around the outside of his horse, and the loop settles around a sagebrush in front of him.

While Charlie shows off, Mr. Piccolo struggles. Mr. Strickland shows him how to swing the loop over his head.

Mr. Piccolo tries swinging the loop, and it knocks his hat to the ground. His second try ends up around his neck. The third spin whacks his horse in the ear. His pony pins his ears back and scowls at Mr. Piccolo.

Finally, Mr. Piccolo gets the hang of swinging the rope. He swings awkwardly but doesn't hit himself or his horse. He practices casting a loop at a sagebrush. The loop lands close, but it is twisted and still misses. Mr. Piccolo tries again, but his rope falls to the ground short of his target.

"Are you sure you want to use ropes?" Mr. Piccolo asks. "How about pistols? Knives? I would even agree to leg wrestling. You would have the advantage there too."

"Ropes," Charlie replies matter-of-factly. "I was pretty good at spellin' in elementary school though. How 'bout a spellin' bee?"

"Ropes it is," Mr. Piccolo says.

"I was afraid ya were fixin' to back out," Charlie says.

"It's five after eight," Mr. Strickland says. "It's time to get this match started."

Charlie whirls his horse around and lopes away from the discussion.

Mr. Piccolo pulls his horse around clumsily and struggles with his reins and coils of rope in his left hand and loop in his right hand.

Charlie's horse slides to a stop and spins around twice clockwise and then spins twice counterclockwise. Charlie presses his spur gently on the left, and his horse dances to the right. He presses on the right, and his horse dances to the left.

Badger wants to applaud the show, but watches silently instead.

"Ready, Charlie?" Mr. Strickland asks.

"I'm ready," Charlie replies.

"Are you ready, Mr. Piccolo?" Mr. Strickland asks.

Mr. Piccolo chuckles nervously and replies, "*Sono pronto.*"

"Come again?"

"I am ready."

"Let the joust begin!" Mr. Strickland yells.

Charlie spurs his horse into action. His horse thunders toward Mr. Piccolo. He swings his loop in time with his horse's gait.

Mr. Piccolo rides much more slowly. As he swings his loop, he knocks his hat off and smacks his horse on the ear. His horse shies and knocks Mr. Piccolo slightly off balance.

The front of Charlie's hat flips up as he approaches the gunslinger.

Mr. Piccolo throws his loop, and it settles around his horse's head.

Charlie throws his loop and feeds coils from his left hand. The loop soars as gracefully as an eagle and settles over Mr. Piccolo. Charlie pulls the slack tight around the Italian's arms and waist. Charlie spins two dallies around his saddle horn. The rope is now securely attached to the saddle, but Charlie can still maneuver his lariat. The cowboy lets his rope slide so it's tight enough to contain Mr. Piccolo but not so tight as to pull the man off his horse.

Mr. Piccolo's mount stops, and Charlie's horse spins around to face Mr. Piccolo.

"Do y'all concede, or do I need to pull ya down?" Charlie asks.

"*Concedo, concedo*," Mr. Piccolo says.

"Y'all concede?" Charlie asks again.

"Yes, I concede." Mr. Piccolo replies.

"Y'all will leave?"

"I will leave," Mr. Piccolo says. "But I am certain my employer will still want you to go away from here."

"Who is yer employer?" Charlie asks.

"I would rather not say."

Charlie pulls back on his reins, and the rope tightens around Mr. Piccolo like a straightjacket, pulling him slightly out of the saddle.

"Mr. Fred Winters! It is Mr. Fred Winters!" Mr. Piccolo yells as he squirms in his binds.

Charlie steps his horse forward, and Mr. Piccolo settles back into his saddle.

"Do y'all know why Mr. Winters wants the Shoesole boys outta here?"

"I never ask," Mr. Piccolo replies.

"I believe that," Charlie says as he unwinds the dallies from around his saddle horn. He shakes some slack into the rope, and Mr. Piccolo crawls out of the loop. He tosses the rope to the ground, and Charlie coils his rope and ties it to his saddle.

"I would get more than a rope," Mr. Piccolo says. "I would guess that Mr. Fred Winters is not going to agree to a rope joust. He will probably come with guns."

"I appreciate yer warnin'," Charlie says. "Yer not so bad after all. Wanna stick around for a while, at least stay for a meal?"

"I need to go break my agreement with Mr. Fred Winters and get back to the mine," Mr. Piccolo says with a shake of his head.

"Well, stop by any time," Charlie says.

Badger's jaw drops. *Charlie is invitin' the man hired to scare us off to stop by anytime. There is no end to his generosity.*

Mr. Piccolo swings his horse around and rides down the trail. And just like that the notorious Sausage Pickle is gone.

THE STEWPOT BOILS WITH lunch. With all the morning excitement, the cowboys have yet to leave the buckaroo wagons. There is work to do, but it is not getting done. But Badger's breakfast was interrupted, so he is as hungry as a badger. The chunks of meat have all turned brown and the potatoes, onions, and carrots are all soft. As Badger walks over to the buckaroo wagon to grab a plate, he notices a cloud of dust in the distance.

Not another rider interruptin' a meal, Badger thinks.

"Do you see the dust?" Badger asks Charlie.

"Yeah, I see it," Charlie says.

"Is that Mr. Winters?" Badger asks.

"I'm not an eagle, Badger," Charlie says. "I can't see that far away. Why don't ya just sit down and eat?"

Badger shakes his head. *I wish Charlie would get just a little bit anxious sometimes.*

Badger levels his plate, and the cook pours a ladle of stew on it. Badger looks for a comfortable spot to sit and finally settles on a patch of grass with a sagebrush as a backrest.

As Badger places his first forkful of meat to his mouth, Mr. Winters pulls up at the buckaroo wagon. He looks angry and rides straight to Charlie.

Everyone stands except for Badger, who takes one more bite before reluctantly setting his plate down and standing. Everyone at the camp looks agitated except for Charlie, who is collected, and Badger, who slowly chews.

"I want Charlie Pickett and all the hands from the Shoesole Ranch outta here," Mr. Winters says. "And I want you outta here now."

Mr. Winters puts his hand on his pistol like a coiled rattlesnake, but he leaves it in the holster.

"We've been expectin' ya, Mr. Winters," Charlie says, "and we know 'bout yer political disagreement with Colonel McGill."

"That's all in the past. The Silver Party just joined with the Democrats. So just like that, me and the colonel are allies," Mr. Winters says.

"Then what's yer problem with Colonel McGill?" Charlie asks.

"My only problem with Colonel McGill is you, Charlie," Mr. Winters spits.

Charlie is taken aback. "I hardly know ya, Mr. Winters," Charlie says. "I'm sorry if I've done somethin' to offend ya."

"You just bein' here offends me," Mr. Winters says, his lip curled. "We don't need your kind here."

"Charlie's kind?" Mr. Strickland says. "Charlie's kind is honest, hardworkin', and the handiest cowboy I know with a horse or rope. We could use more folks like Charlie—and fewer folks like you, Fred."

"A movin' speech, Homer," Mr. Winters says, "but it doesn't change anythin'. This territory isn't big enough for both Charlie and me."

All the cowboys milling around the buckaroo wagon move closer to Charlie. They fill in the gaps around and behind Charlie until it is abundantly clear that everyone is standing with Charlie.

Mr. Winters pulls his pistol and points it at Charlie. Mr. Winter's horse circles nervously. The angry cowboy pulls back on the reins, and his horse stops but throws his head in protest.

"Now listen," Charlie says. "Mr. Winters' problem is with me and me alone."

"That's not true, Charlie," Badger says as he walks to the front of the crowd and stands between Charlie and Mr. Winters. "Charlie, you told me you gotta stand up to a bully, and you have stood up to every bully who has come through here. And you told me it's easier to stand up to a bully if you have somebody standin' with you."

"I appreciate that," Charlie says, "but I don't need ya to fight my fights for me."

As the tension builds, Mr. Winters squeezes his horse tighter with his knees and pulls the reins tighter. The rancher and his sorrel circle again, but Mr. Winters is quickly losing control of his mount. His bronc rears up on its hind legs.

Mr. Winters tries to holster his pistol but drops it instead. With both hands free, he grabs the reins and tries to calm his horse. His mount bogs his head and pulls the rancher forward.

The horse lunges, bucks twice, and Mr. Winters face plants on the ground, catching his foot in a stirrup on the way down. Mr. Winters' leg is high in the air, trapped to the saddle while the rest of him is plastered to the ground. The horse circles uneasily.

"I'm caught!" Mr. Winters hollers. "I'm hung up! Someone help me, please."

"Shoot your pistol, Homer, and his horse will run," a cowboy yells from the crowd. "That'd kill him."

"No," Charlie says calmly but forcefully. "Nobody's killin' Mr. Winters."

Mr. Winters looks up at Charlie with eyes like a cross between a scared rabbit and a confused puppy. Charlie walks up to Mr. Winters' horse. He holds out his hand, and the scared horse tentatively sniffs his fingers. Charlie touches the horse's nose and then scratches the

horse between his ears. With a touch from Charlie, the horse calms down and stands still.

Charlie pulls out his knife and walks to the horse's shoulder.

"Don't hurt me!" Mr. Winters cries as he looks up at Charlie. Hung up in his stirrup, the rancher is very vulnerable.

Charlie smiles as he presses his knife against a strap on the stirrup leather. The strap cuts and unravels from the stirrup. The stirrup falls from the saddle, and Mr. Winters' leg drops to the ground.

The gray-haired cowboy lies on the ground shaking with fear as Charlie stands over him. Charlie calmly puts his knife away. He reaches down and offers a hand up to Mr. Winters, who hesitantly accepts the help.

Charlie looks at all the cowboys at the buckaroo wagon and says, "Boys, I don't hate Mr. Winters." Charlie has his arm around Mr. Winters as he limps to the wagons. "My pa was born a slave down in Texas, but he died a free man. He saw a lot of hate in his lifetime. But he always told me, 'Hate begets hate. Only love can stop hate.'"

The cowboys stand silently and kick the dirt as Charlie explains, "I can't stop Mr. Winters from hatin' me by hatin' him back. That doesn't solve anythin'. But I can show him respect and mercy, and only that can change Mr. Winters' heart."

Charlie helps Mr. Winters sit down. Badger grabs a cup of coffee and hands it to the old cowboy. Charlie nods and grins at Badger. Mr. Winters drinks the coffee, but keeps a nervous eye on Charlie.

"I'm not gonna hurt ya, Mr. Winters," Charlie says. "I'm gonna give ya some coffee and lunch. And I'm gonna offer ya help fixin' yer saddle and gettin' home."

"Why are you doin' this?" Mr. Winters asks. "I hate you?" Mr. Winters says reluctantly, beginning to question his own words.

"It would be real easy to hate ya back. That's how we got to this spot in the first place—our ancestors hatin' one another, fearin' one another. But it stops right now, today—with me. Because I won't hate ya back."

Mr. Winters looks at Charlie, still confused. "I don't know what to say."

"Y'all don't have to say anythin'. In my mind, it's over."

"I could use that help gettin' home," Mr. Winters says.

"I'll send Gib with ya," Charlie says.

Gib jumps up and brings Mr. Winters' horse and his own over. The young cowboy helps the injured rancher mount, and together they ride away with a confused Mr. Winters looking back over his shoulder.

Charlie waves goodbye.

"Why'd you do that?" Badger asks. "He can get healed up and just come after you again."

"I know, Badger. But bullies aren't born; they're made," Charlie says. "Most of the time, the only thing a bully ever knows is hate. Maybe their parents bully 'em or some other bully comes into their life. If we can show a little love, then maybe, just maybe they can learn that instead."

"So you're not worried?" Badger asks.

"Well, I can't pull a string and make Mr. Winters change," Charlie says. "But I can treat him like all people should be treated. That's all we can do. And as far as worry, I don't have time to worry. We've got work to do."

"So what do we do now?" Badger asks.

"Well, we wasted a whole mornin' talkin' and carryin' on," Charlie says. "I say we get back to what we do best."

"You mean we get back to the rodeo?" Badger says.

"That right," Charlie says. "Let's rodeo."

Glossary

bronc/bronco—a horse with a tendency to buck when ridden.

buck—the act of a horse attempting to dislodge their rider. The horse will jump and kick to accomplish his goal.

bull—a male bovine. Male cattle.

burr—the prickly outside of a flowered plant.

cantle—the back of the saddle

chaps—leather legging worn by cowboys

colt—a young horse

cow paddies—cow manure; cow poop.

crow hops—a weak bucking action. The horse jumps but doesn't kick above its flank.

cud—the bolus a ruminant regurgitates for further chewing.

dally—the act of spinning a rope around a saddle horn to secure it to a saddle.

dinks—small calves

drag—the tail end of a herd.

flanker—one who works at the flank or side of an animal. In this context, a cowboy who holds a rope to allow a rider to mount his horse.

foal—a baby horse

game—a wild animal that can be hunted for food.

greenhorn—a rookie; a novice.

hardtack—a hard biscuit popularized by the Union Army during the Civil War.

hobbles—a leather strap that can be buckled around a horse's feet to prevent free movement.

lariat—a long, small rope with a honda used for catching cattle and horses.

latigo—the leather strap that secures a saddle to a horse.

lek—a playa where sagegrouse preform their mating dance.

mugger—usually a team of cowboys that wrestle an animal to the ground.

remuda—a herd of saddle horses.

rope—the act of throwing a lariat around a part of a horse or cow to catch the animal.

saddle horn—a post on the front of a saddle used to attach a rope to the saddle.

slick calf—an unbranded calf.

waddle—a piece of hide that is cut to hang. It is used for ownership identification.

wild rag—a large, silk scarf used by cowboys.

From the author...

Badger Thurston and the Trouble at the Rodeo is a work of fiction. But parts of the story actually happened. The book's Charlie Pickett is based on the real-life Henry Harris, a cowboy who rode the ranges of Southern Idaho and Northern Nevada. Henry was born in Georgetown, Texas, on December 15, 1865, just after the 13th Amendment to the Constitution was ratified, which freed slaves in the United States. Henry's parents had been slaves in Texas.

When Henry was a teenager, he moved to Nevada to work as a house servant for John Sparks. But Henry spent more time riding and roping than he did in the house. John recognized Henry's talent with horses and helped him become a cowboy. As good as Henry was with horses, he was even better with people. John Sparks eventually promoted Henry to cowboss, putting him in charge of a ranch and buckaroo wagon with fourteen cowboys reporting to him. With Henry's help, Mr. Sparks owned and cared for 75,000 head of cattle on more than 2 million acres of land in Southern Idaho and Northeastern Nevada.

Henry was well-respected and known as one of the handiest cowboys to ride the ranges. In the 1930s, Henry moved to Cedar Creek, Idaho, where he taught several young cowboys the techniques of their trade. One of those young cowboys was my grandfather.

Henry died in 1937. In 2008, Henry was inducted into the Buckaroo Hall of Fame and, in 2009, the Cowboys of Color Hall of Fame.

About the author...

Gus Brackett was raised on a working cattle ranch in the wide open spaces of Southwestern Idaho and Northeastern Nevada. He was on the back of a horse by the age of five and sold his first steer at the age of ten. Gus was enrolled in a one-room school house where he first started writing stories about cowboys.

As a boy, Gus listened to tall tales about early cowboys from Grandpa Noy Brackett, Uncle Rolly Patrick and Truman Clark. Gus was fascinated by these stories and started writing the Badger Thurston series in 2010 to chronicle these tales.

Gus currently lives and works on the same ranch where he was raised. He is the Chairman of the Board of the one room school where he first wrote cowboy stories. He lives in a little ranch house with his wife Kimberly, four children, and a barn full of horses, steers, dogs, cats, and chickens. He is still writing so look for other books in this series.

If you enjoyed this Badger Thurston book, you will enjoy the other books in the Badger Thurston series. It's the year 1910. Badger Thurston is an ordinary kid, but trouble seems to find him wherever he goes...as a cowboy, as a teamster, and as a flunkie on a construction site.

The Badger Thurston books will be enjoyed by the whole family. Action, adventure, mystery...these easy reading books will spark your interest in the Old West.

Badger Thurston and the Cattle Drive
Badger Thurston and the Runaway Stagecoach
Badger Thurston and the Mud Pits
Badger Thurston and the Trouble at the Rodeo

Watch for the next book in this series.

Order your copy today at:
www.badgerthurston.com or on **Amazon.com**.

Or send a check or money order for $10.25 plus $3.50 for shipping and handling to:

12 Baskets Book Publishing
54899 Crawfish Rd.
Rogerson ID 83302

Made in the USA
Columbia, SC
13 November 2018